Colors of Compassion: The Artivism of Lila Marquez

Copyright © Lila Marquez
Kuwait 2021

ISBN: 978-1-716-58157-1

ALL RIGHTS RESERVED. No part of this publication may be reproduced, stored in or introduced into a retrieval system, or transmitted, in any form, or by any means (electronic, mechanical, photocopying, recording or otherwise without the prior written permission of the author or publisher.

Printed by Lulu Press
February 2021

Lines of Lila Online Art Gallery
www.linesoflila.com

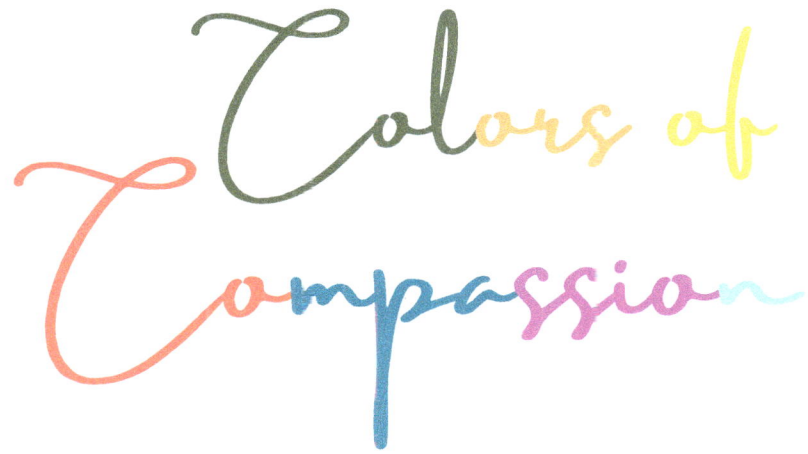

THE ARTIVISM OF LILA MARQUEZ

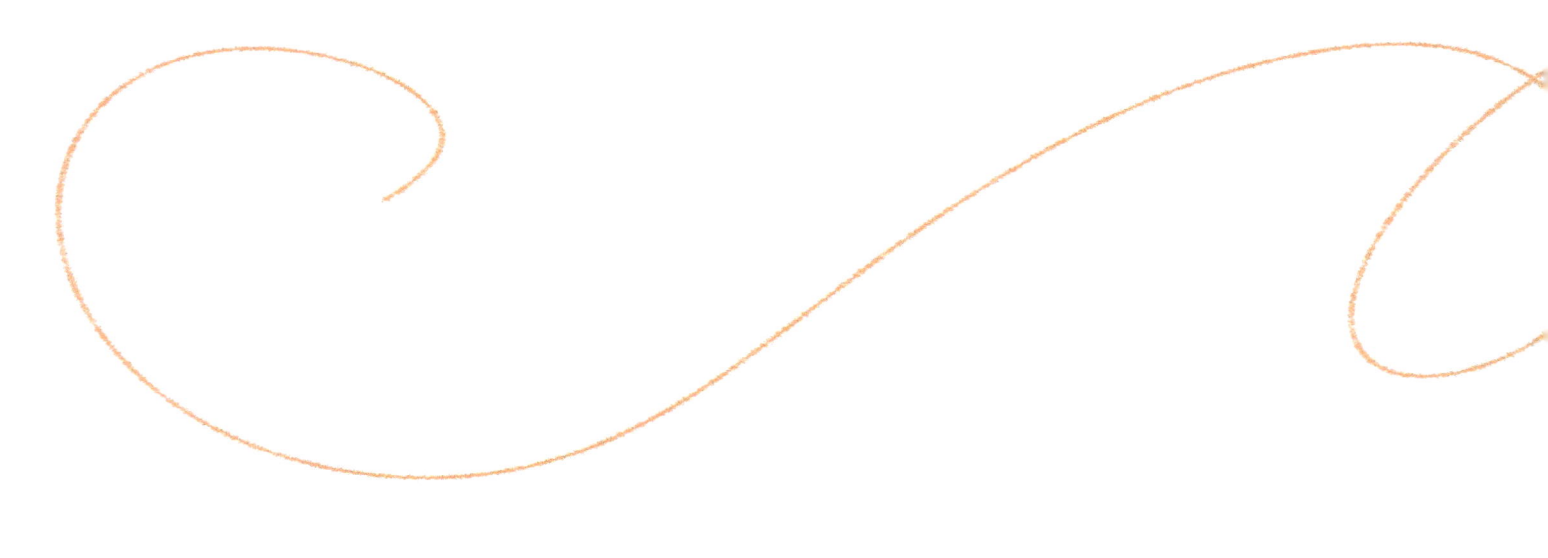
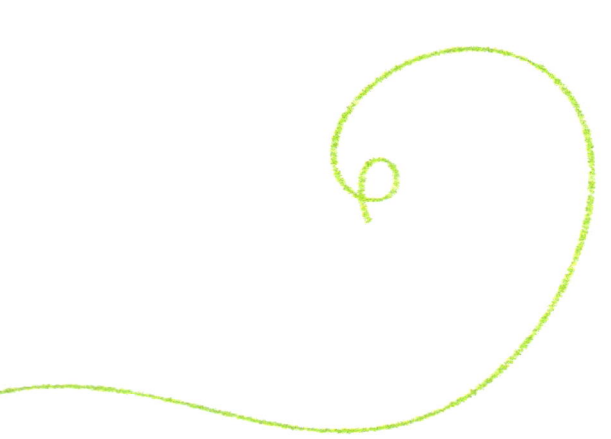

## ACKNOWLEDGMENTS

First and foremost, I would like to thank my family for supporting me in my artistic journey and for being by my side throughout my vegan advocacy.

I'm also expressing how grateful I am for having the chance to share my vegan advocacy through art with the Art of Compassion Project, an international collective of vegan artists dedicated to spreading the message of kindess and justice for nonhuman animals.

Last but not least, I would like to thank all vegans for your unswerving dedication for animal emancipation.

## FOREWORD

When I began creating art for animal rights and veganism, I had set my mind on making a contribution to the vegan movement by spreading the message of nonviolence and animal emancipation in my own little way.

This book wishes to shed light on animal identity and personhood. It also stands as my statement against animal husbandry and exploitation, with portraits depicting farmed animals or animals in captivity.

I believe that as humans, we should work towards abolishing the oppressive system that we have created for nonhuman animals. By acknowledging that they, too, are people, persons, with personality, needs and emotions, humans will eventually cease from treating them as mere commodity.

In this book, I have compiled my ongoing series of artworks wherein nonhuman animals are depicted as people, with hopes of encouraging its readers to respect their individual autonomy.

## ABOUT THE ARTIST

Lila Marquez is a Filipina writer and artist. She studied Comparative Literature in the Philippines and worked as a professional writer and editor in several niche publications in Kuwait where she lived for over 15 years.

Her articles, columns and illustrations have been published in Kuwait's local newspapers and magazines from 2007 under the pseudonym, Armineonila M. Her literary writings and artworks have also appeared in literary anthologies and art publications in Kuwait and abroad.

For two years now, Lila has been a contributing artist and member of the Art of Compassion Project, an international collective of vegan artists dedicated to spreading animal rights advocacy and the vegan ideology through art.

## TABLE OF CONTENTS

12 *Not Your Toy*

14 *Less Loved*

14 *Commodified*

16 *Captive Seas*

18 *Animals are People, Too*

20 *A Mother's Love*

21 *Blood on the Nest*

22 *Milking Innocence*

23 *Mayumi*

25 *Free Inmate Perla*

## TABLE OF CONTENTS

26 *Paul Deserves to Live*

27 *Lex Deserves to Live*

29 *In a Better Place*

31 *Gentle Lullabies*

31 *Waiting for a Better Home*

33 *Remembering Alf*

34 *Hope for the Animals*

36 *Cageless*

37 *Sketches*

43 *Break Away*

47 *Exhibitions*

To Badlis, Koolit, Bunchkin, Tisoy, Tisay, Brownie, Faloos, Nica, Richard, Parker, Alfie, Noonah, Choco, Luna, Bambi...

You are in my heart forever.

Creating line paintings on animals has made me realize that art is a powerful tool for change. This book is a testament that creative activism has a special place in the vegan advocacy.

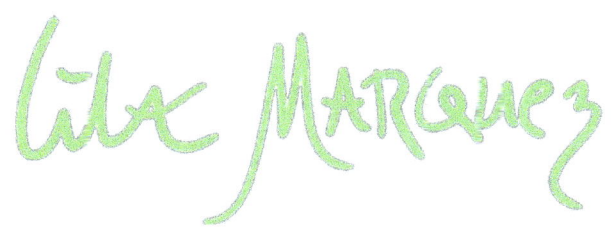

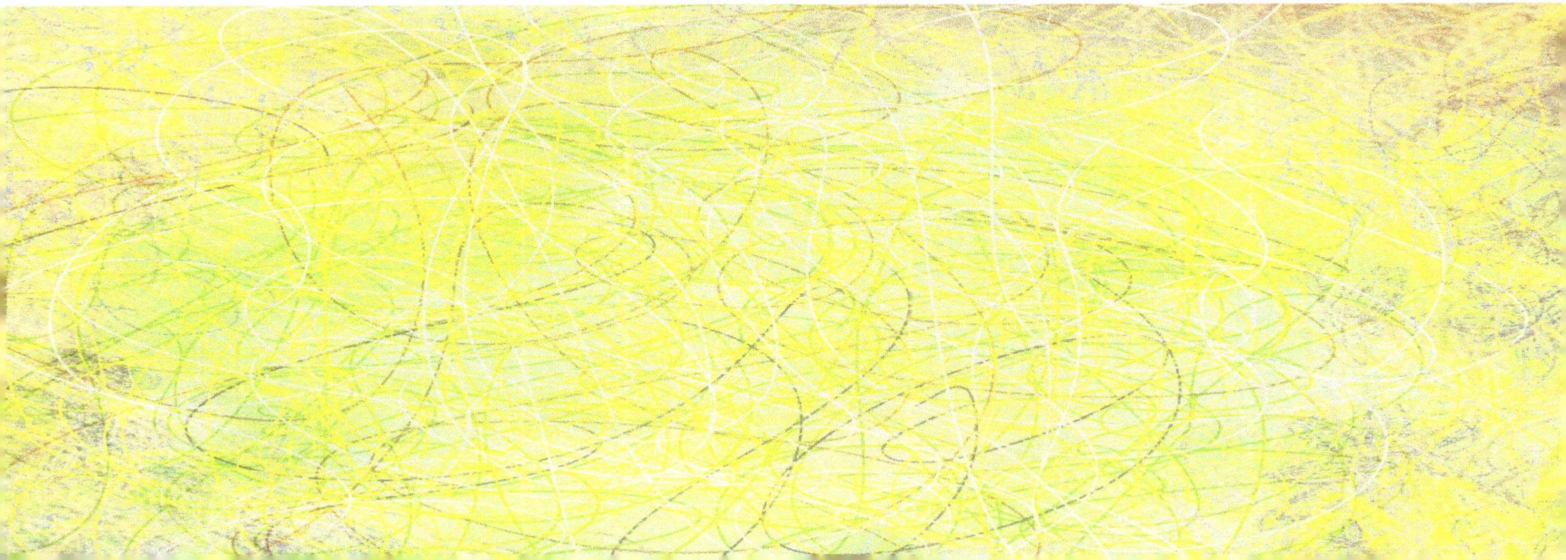

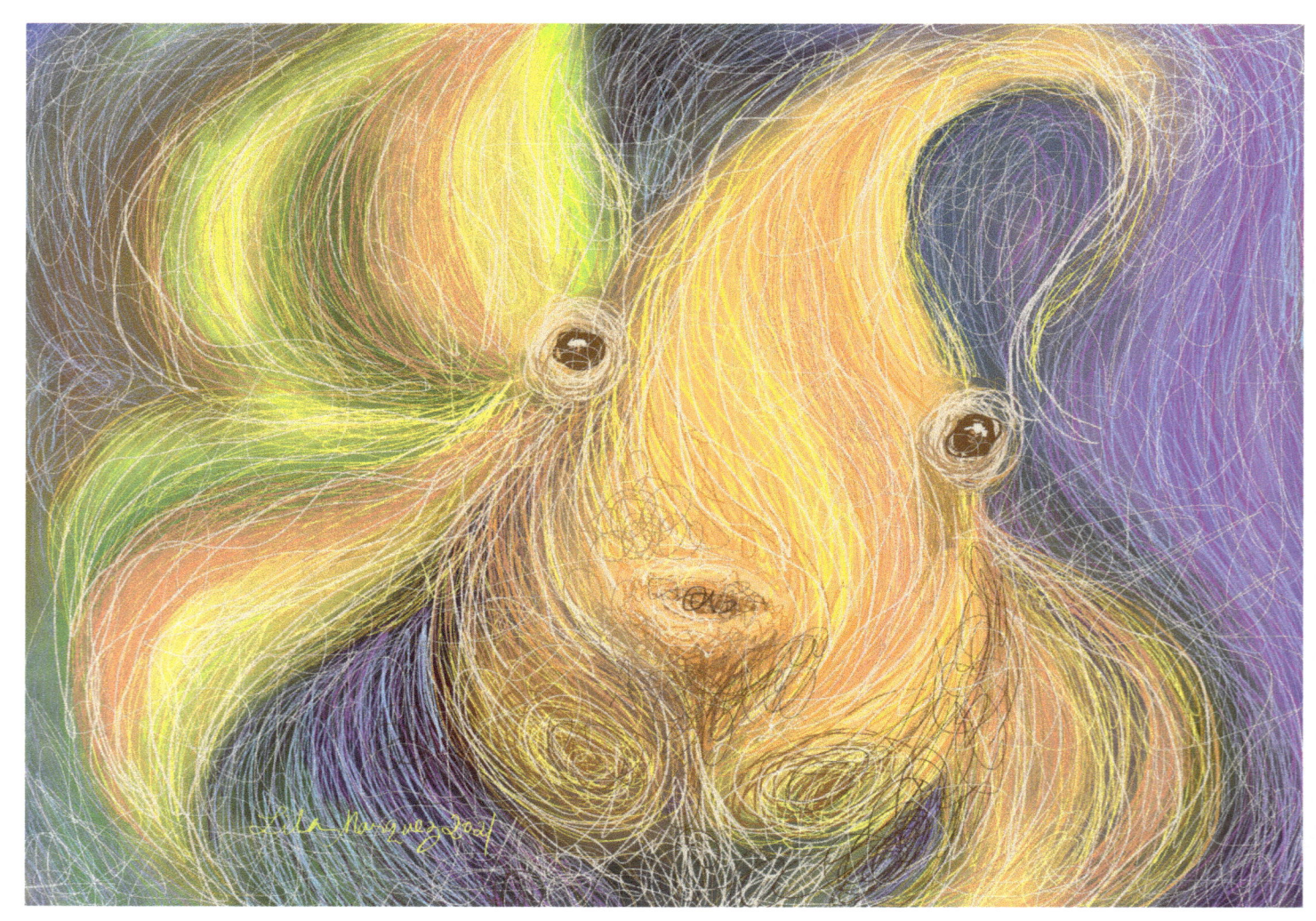

NOT YOUR TOY
20 x 16 in

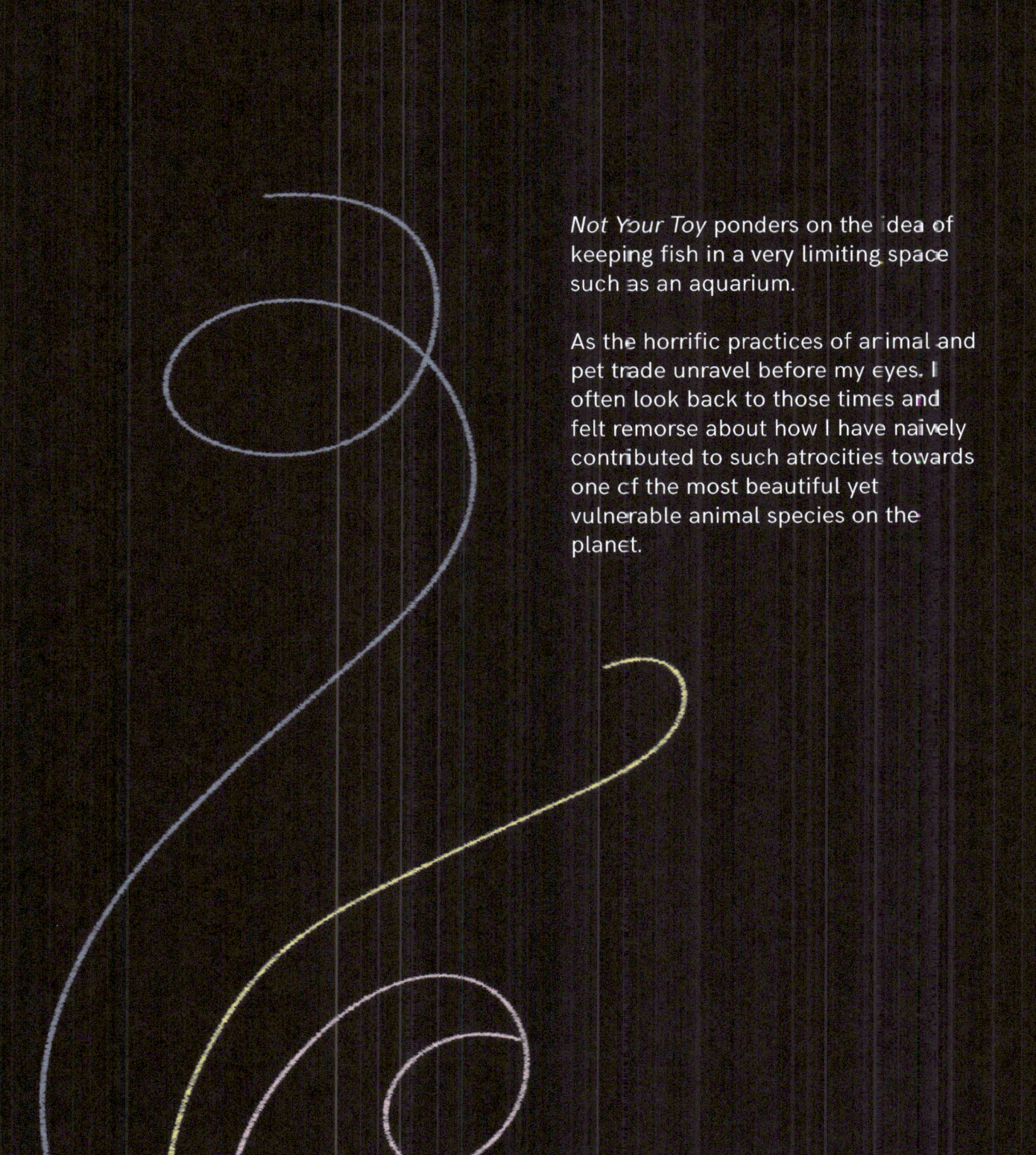

*Not Your Toy* ponders on the idea of keeping fish in a very limiting space such as an aquarium.

As the horrific practices of animal and pet trade unravel before my eyes. I often look back to those times and felt remorse about how I have naively contributed to such atrocities towards one of the most beautiful yet vulnerable animal species on the planet.

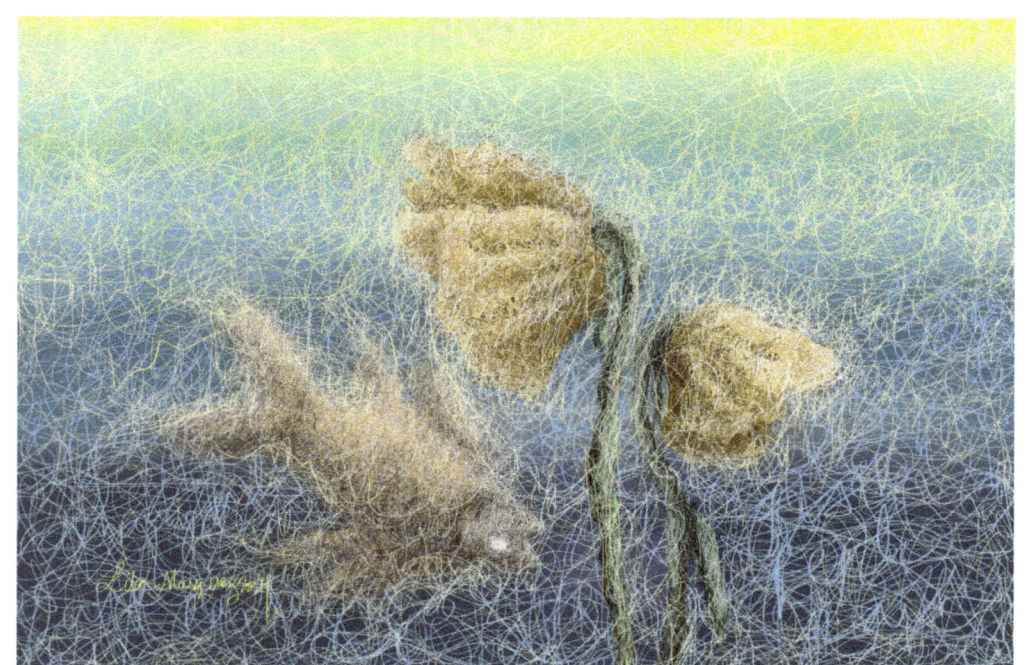

LESS LOVED
30 x 20 in

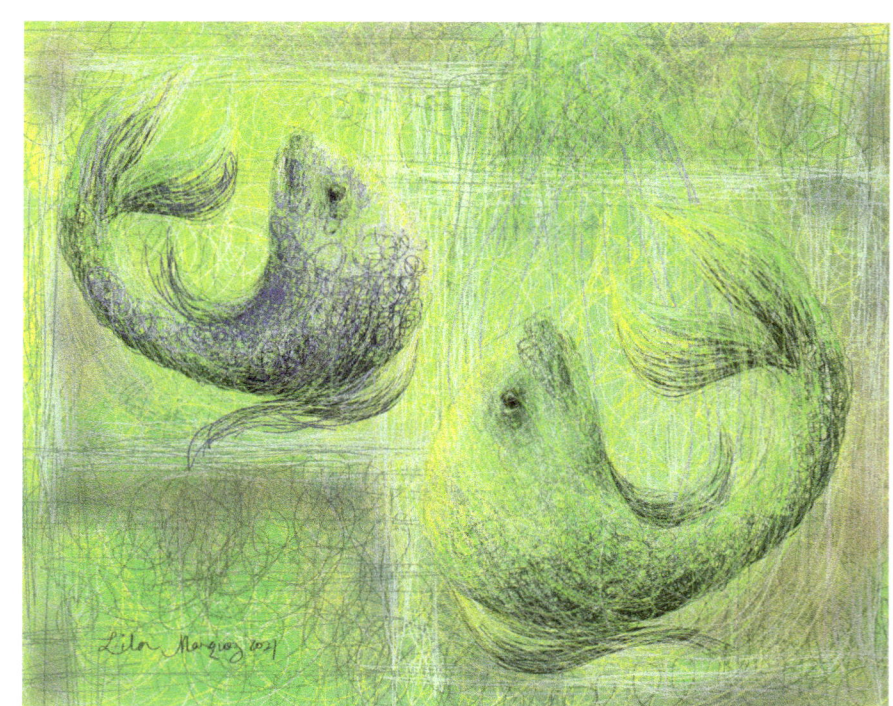

COMMODIFIED
20 x 16 in

The exploitation of marine animals is one of the many animal rights issues often pushed to the back burner. This is because the cognitive faculties of most of the ocean's organisms are being put to question to this day, making them an ideal target for horrific oppression by the animal agribusiness.

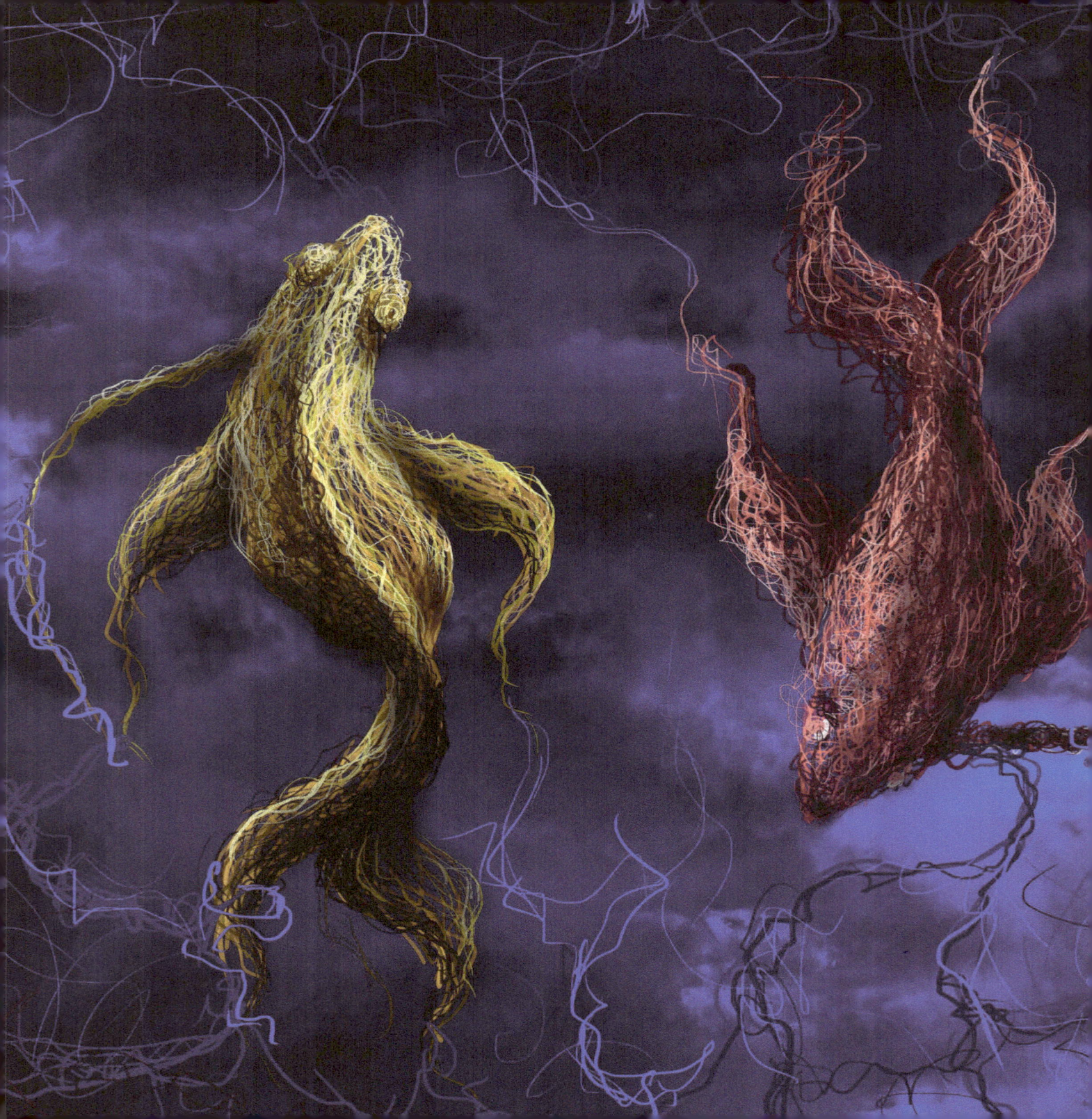

CAPTIVE SEAS
23.4 x 16.5 in

*Captive Seas* is one of my personal favorites among my animal-themed art pieces as it emotionally speaks to me. I hope that this artwork speaks to more compassionate people, too.

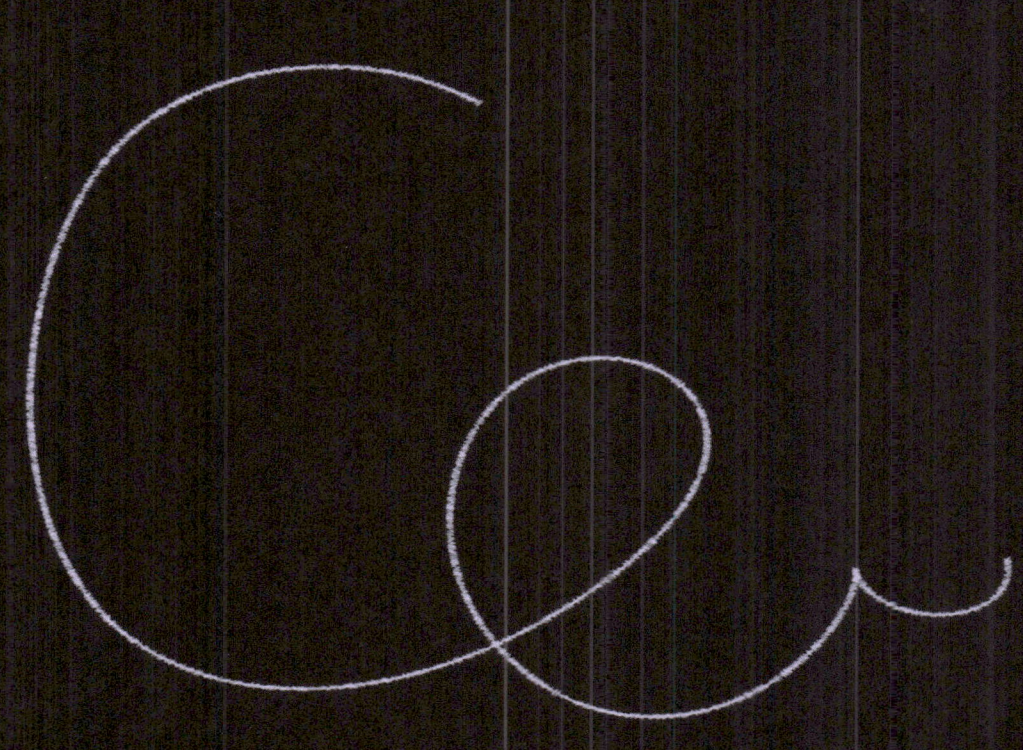

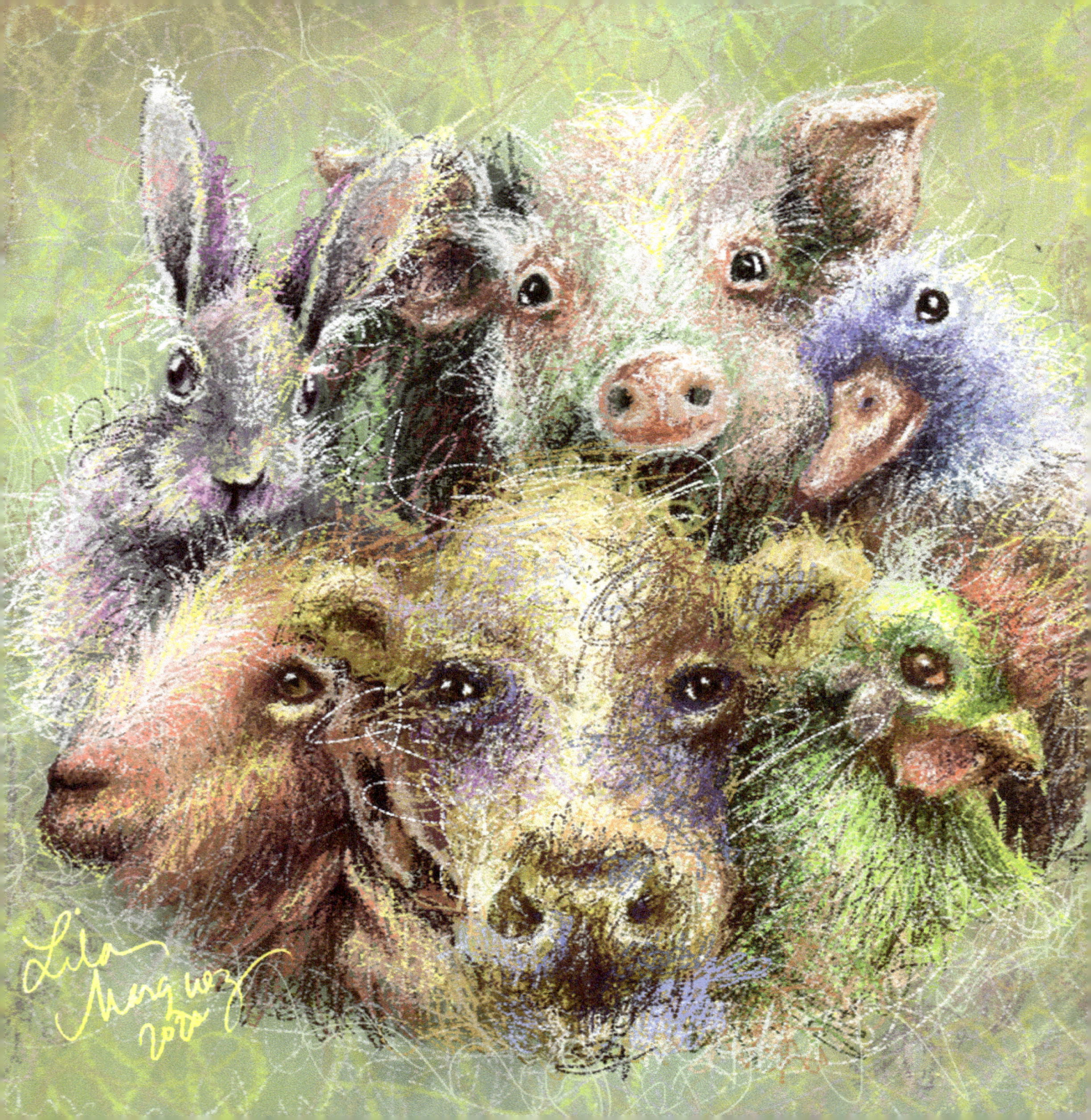

ANIMALS ARE PEOPLE, TOO
11 x 8.5 in

*Animals Are People, Too* is my tribute to farm animals. It is also my statement against animal husbandry and slavery. I believe that us, humans, should work towards their emancipation from the oppressive system we have created for them. By acknowledging that nonhuman animals are people, persons, with personality, needs and emotions, humans will eventually cease from treating them as mere commodity.

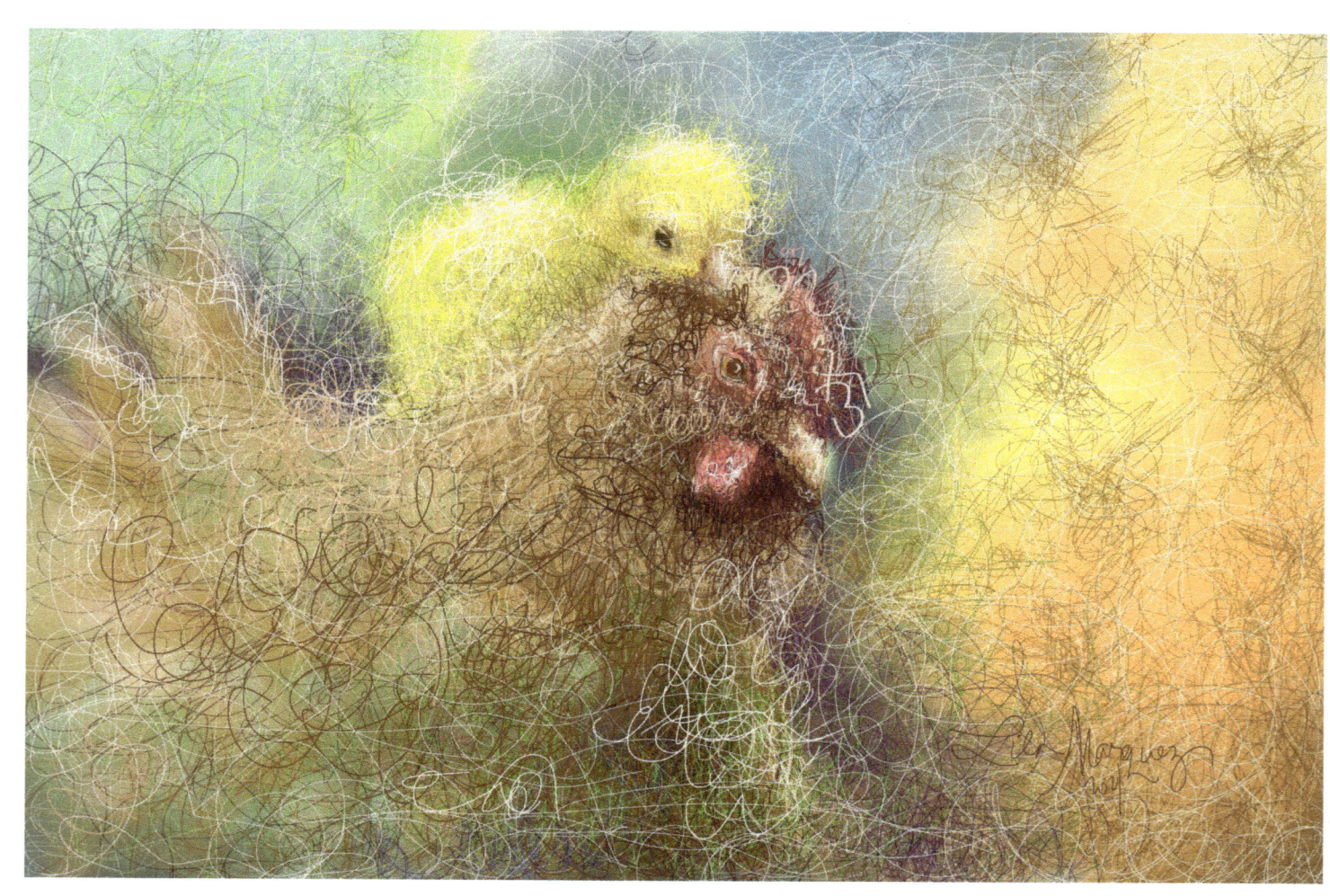

A MOTHER'S LOVE
30 x 20 in

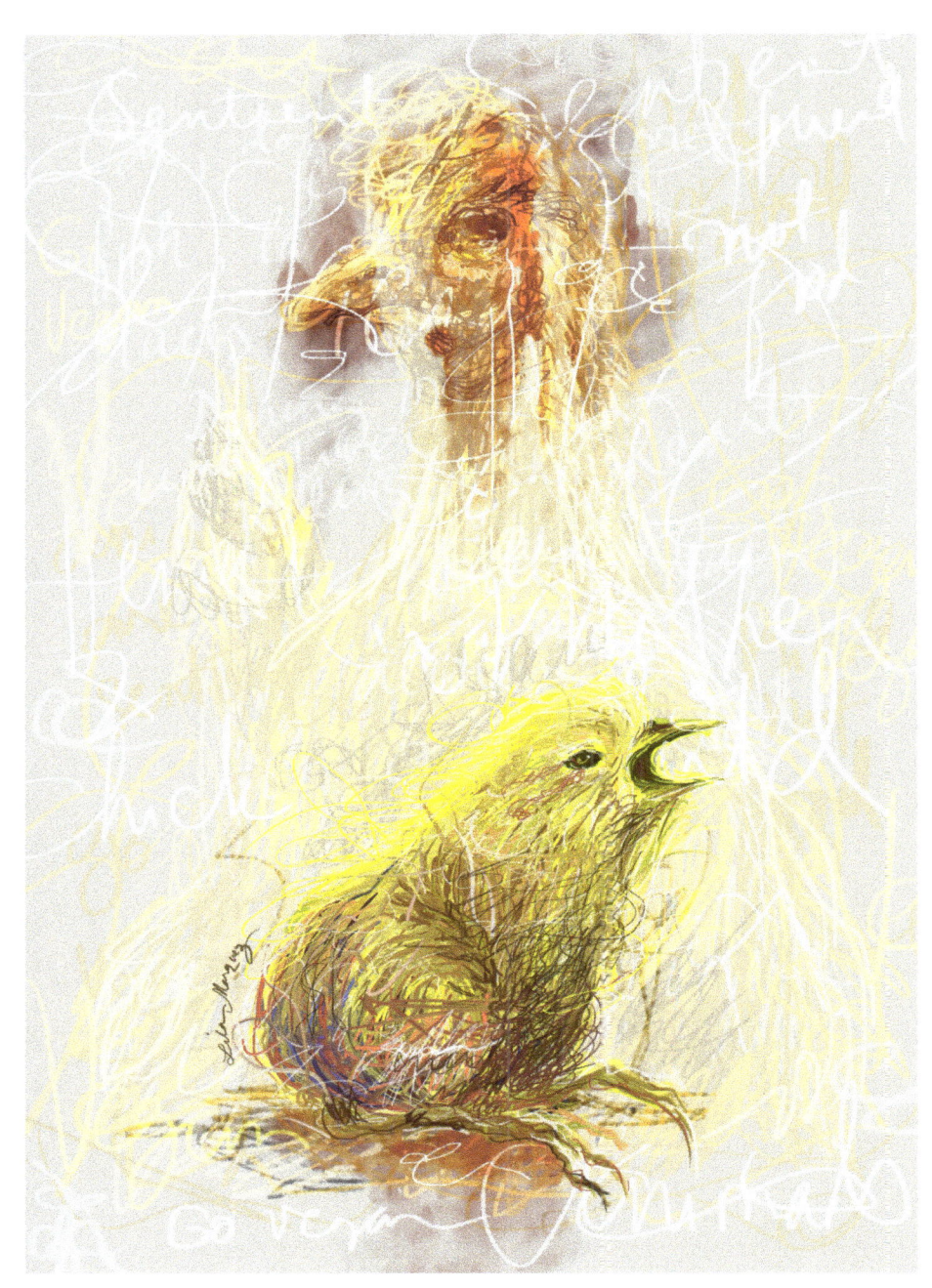

BLOOD ON THE NEST
11.69 x 16.53 in

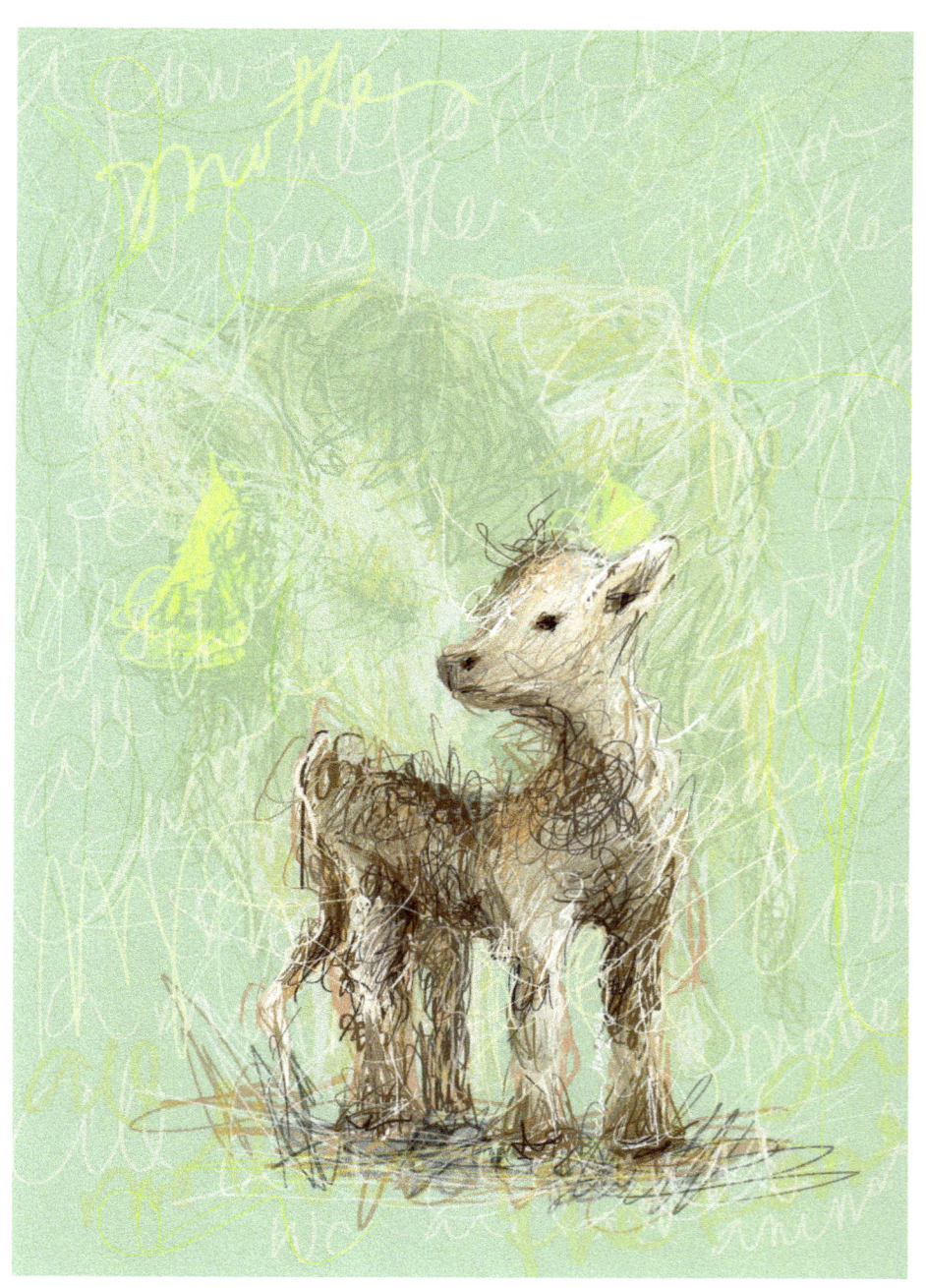

MILKING INNOCENCE
11.69 x 16.53 in

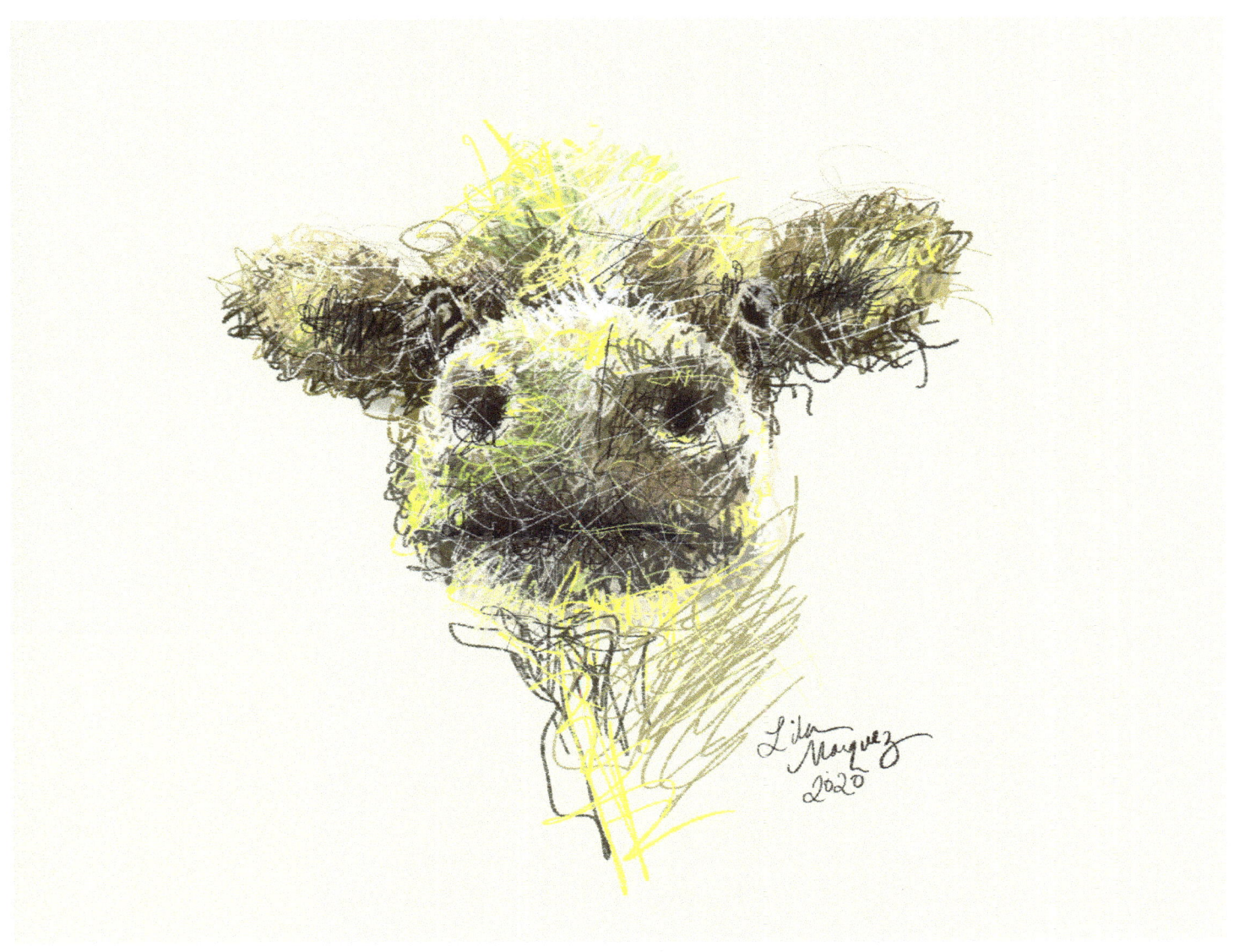

MAYUMI
11 x 8.5 in

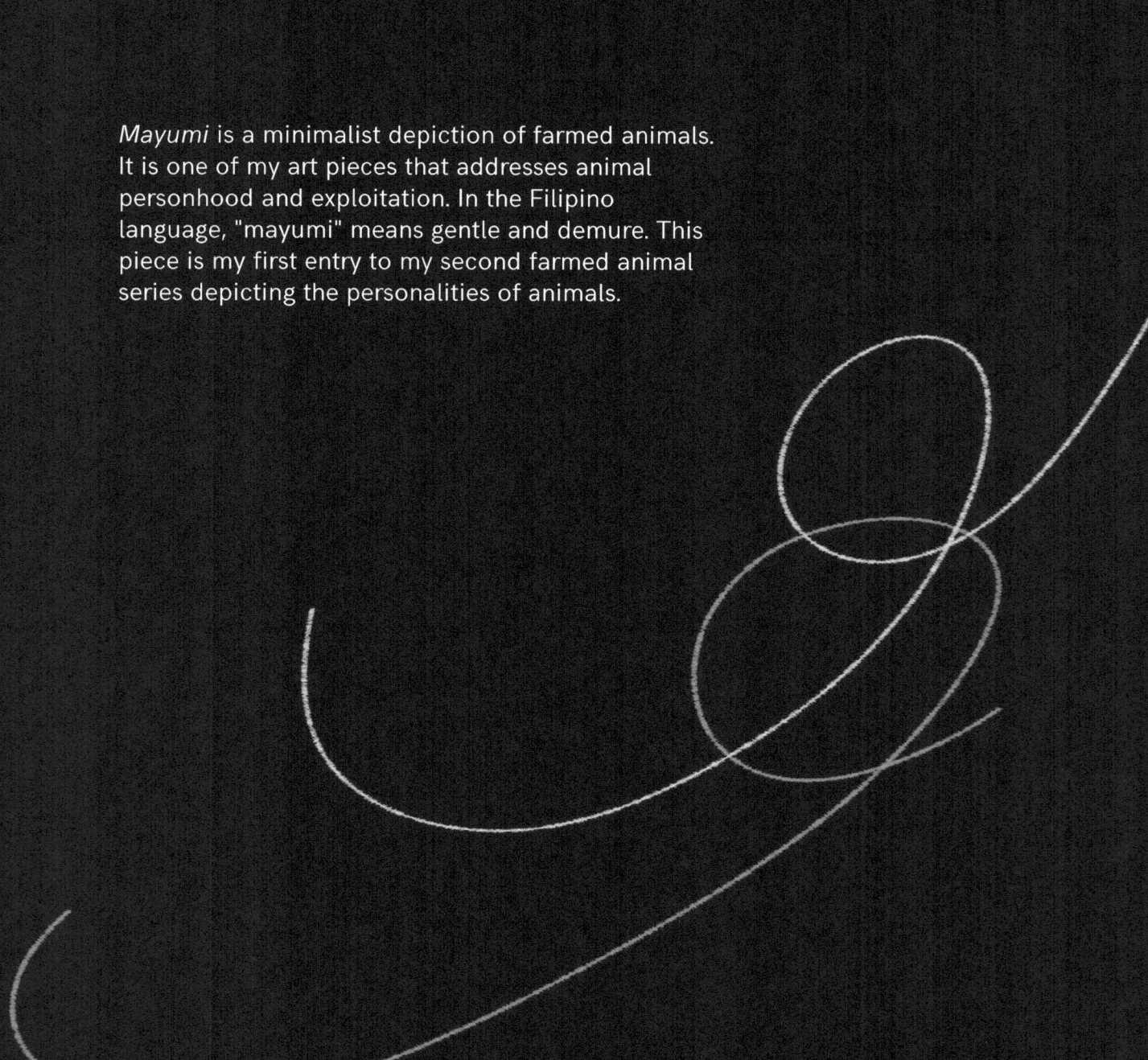

*Mayumi* is a minimalist depiction of farmed animals. It is one of my art pieces that addresses animal personhood and exploitation. In the Filipino language, "mayumi" means gentle and demure. This piece is my first entry to my second farmed animal series depicting the personalities of animals.

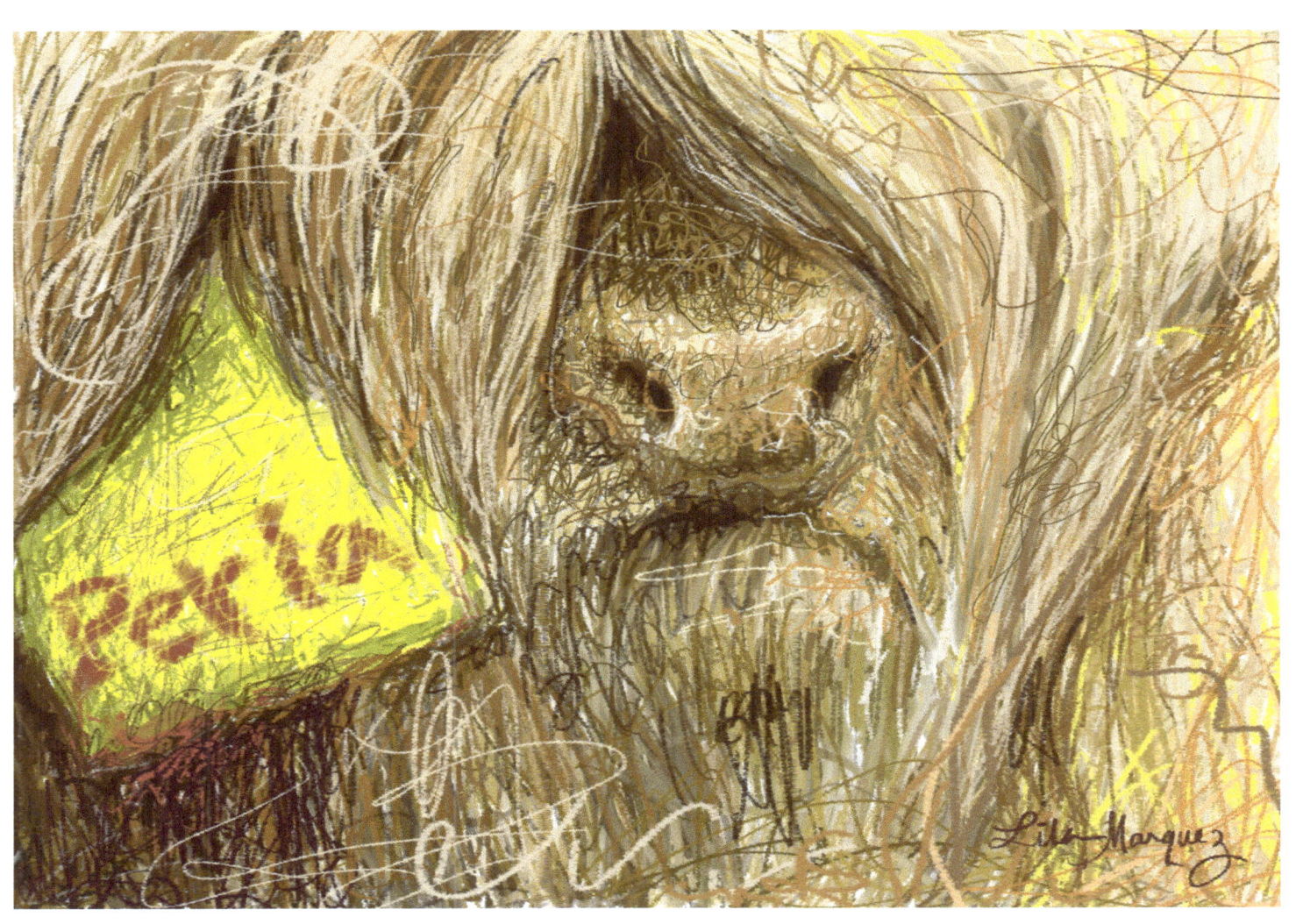

FREE INMATE PERLA
23.4 x 16.5 in

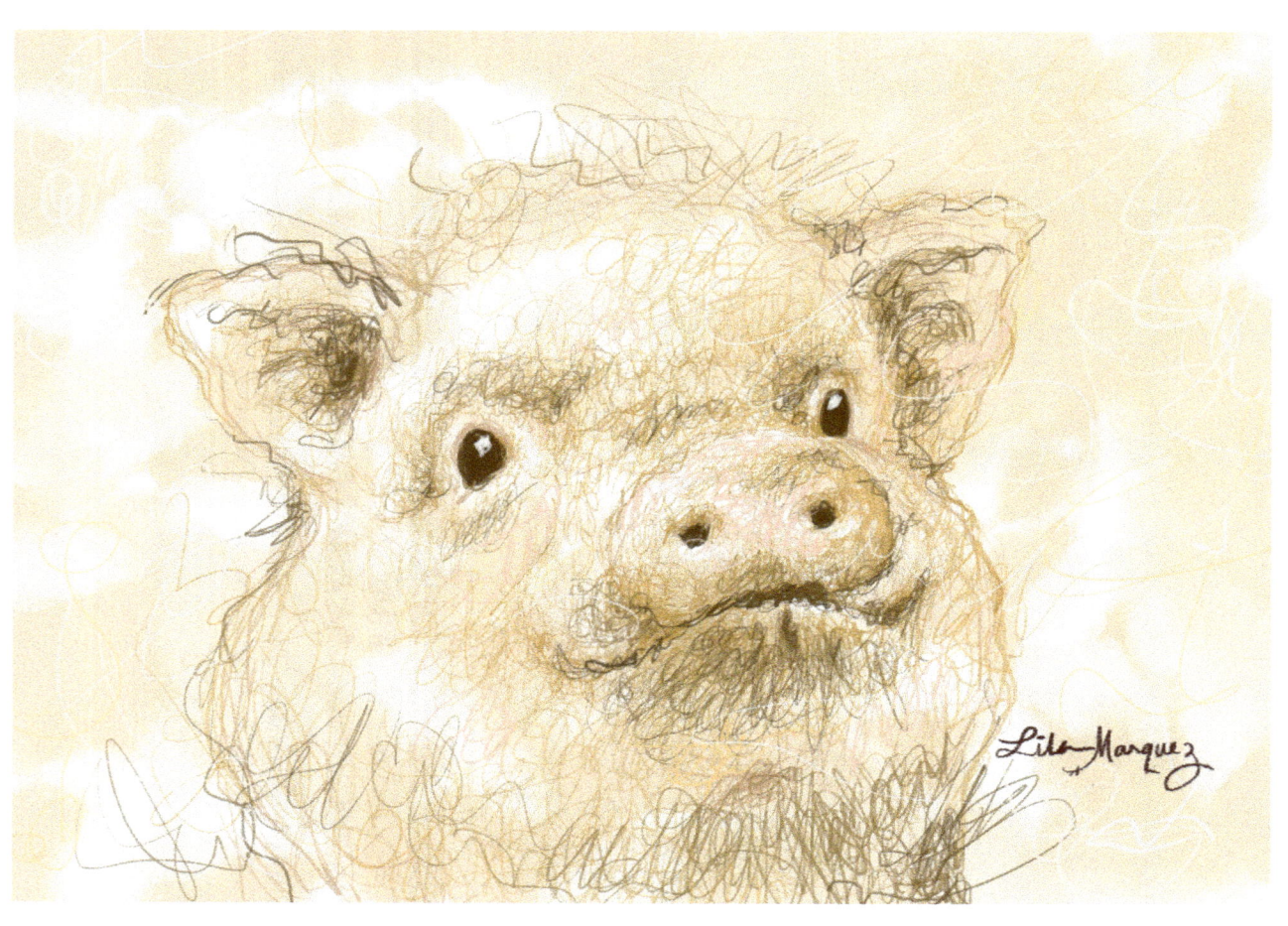

PAUL DESERVES TO LIVE
23.4 x 16.5 in

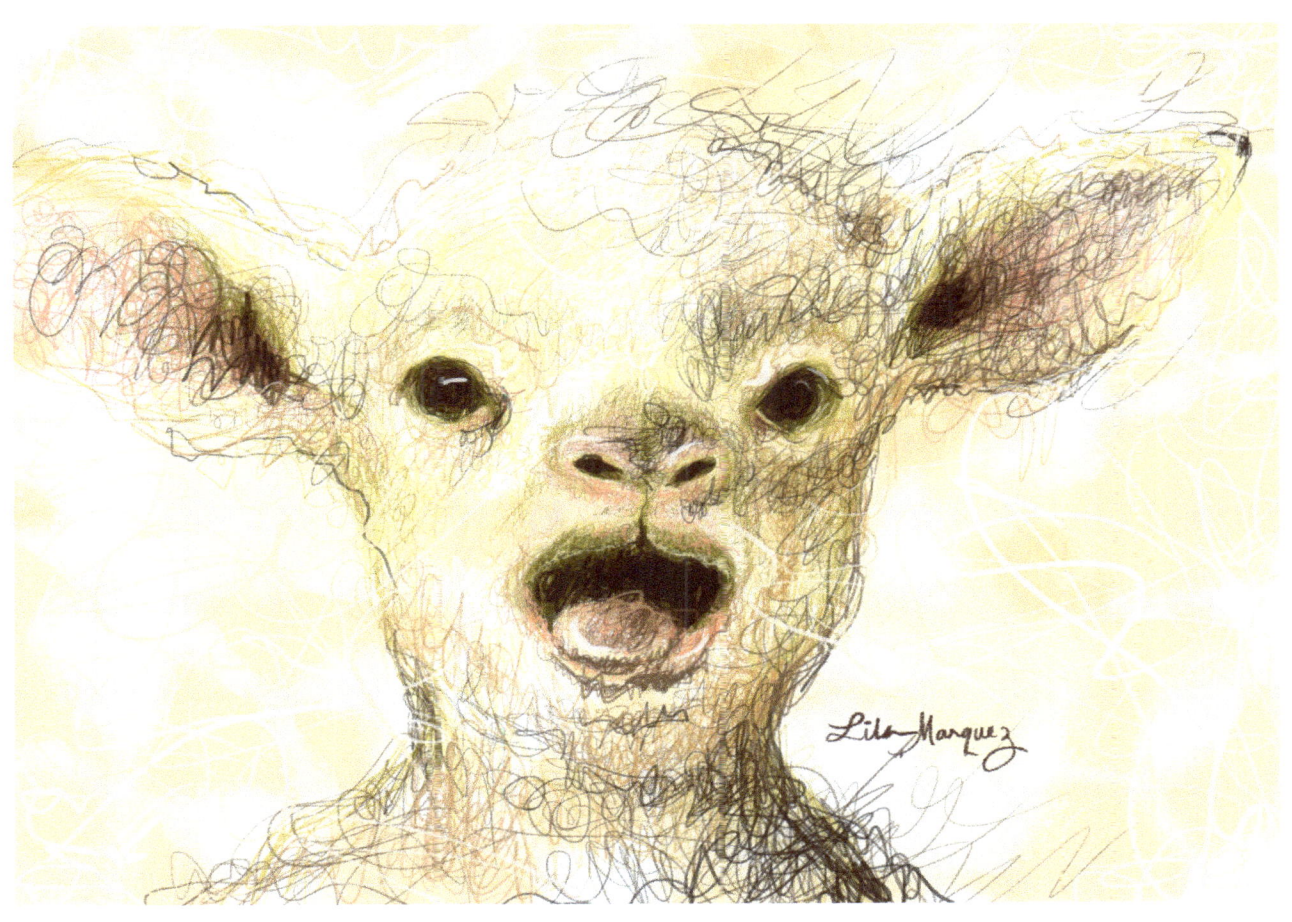

LEX DESERVES TO LIVE
23.4 x 16.5 in

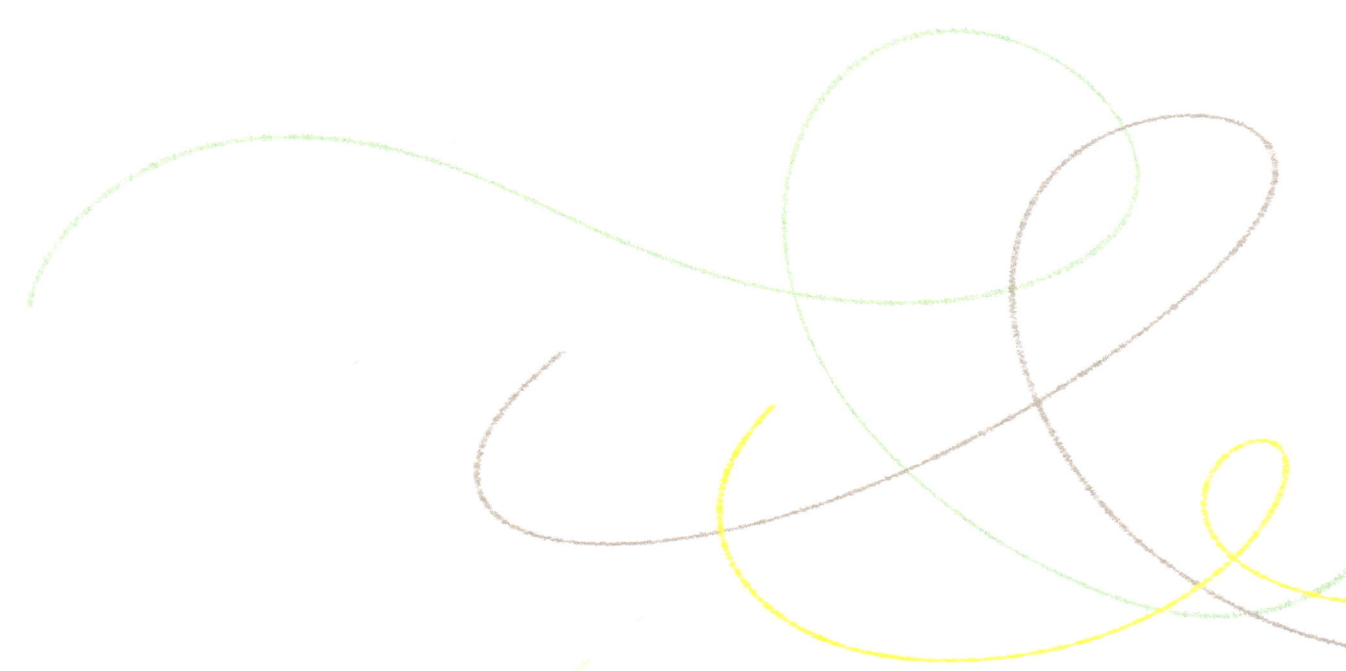

*Lex Deserves to Live* and *Paul Deserves to Live* are digital paintings. These two artworks had personal significance in my younger years. I named them accordingly during my personal interactions with them. They played a pivotal role in my interest in animal rights that lead up to my transition to veganism.

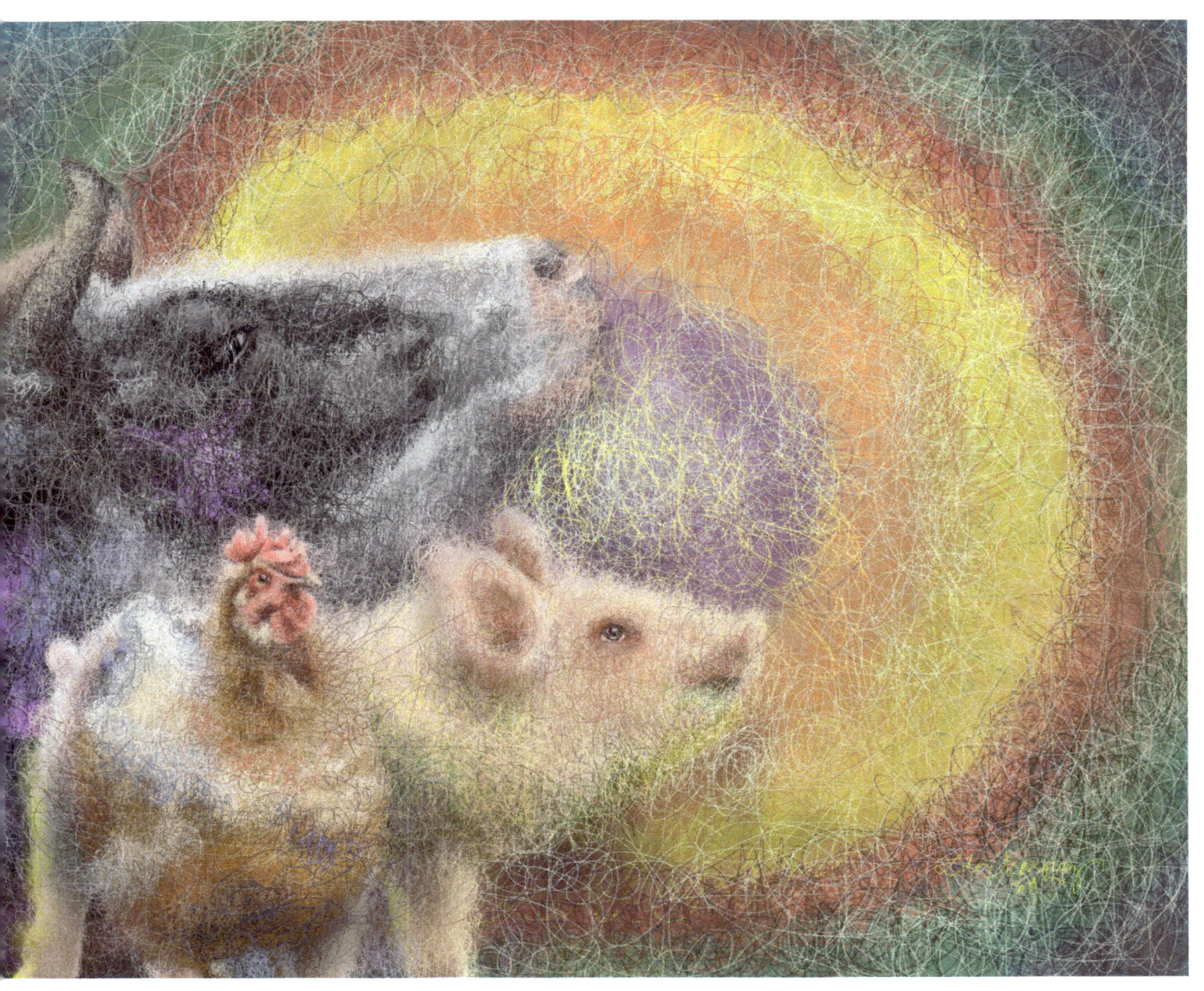

IN A BETTER PLACE
30 x 20 in

A personal favorite of mine, *In a Better Place* depicts my vision for animal emancipation. It embodies all that I have longed for since transitioning to veganism some ten years ago. I'm certain that my vegan colleagues feel the same way, too.

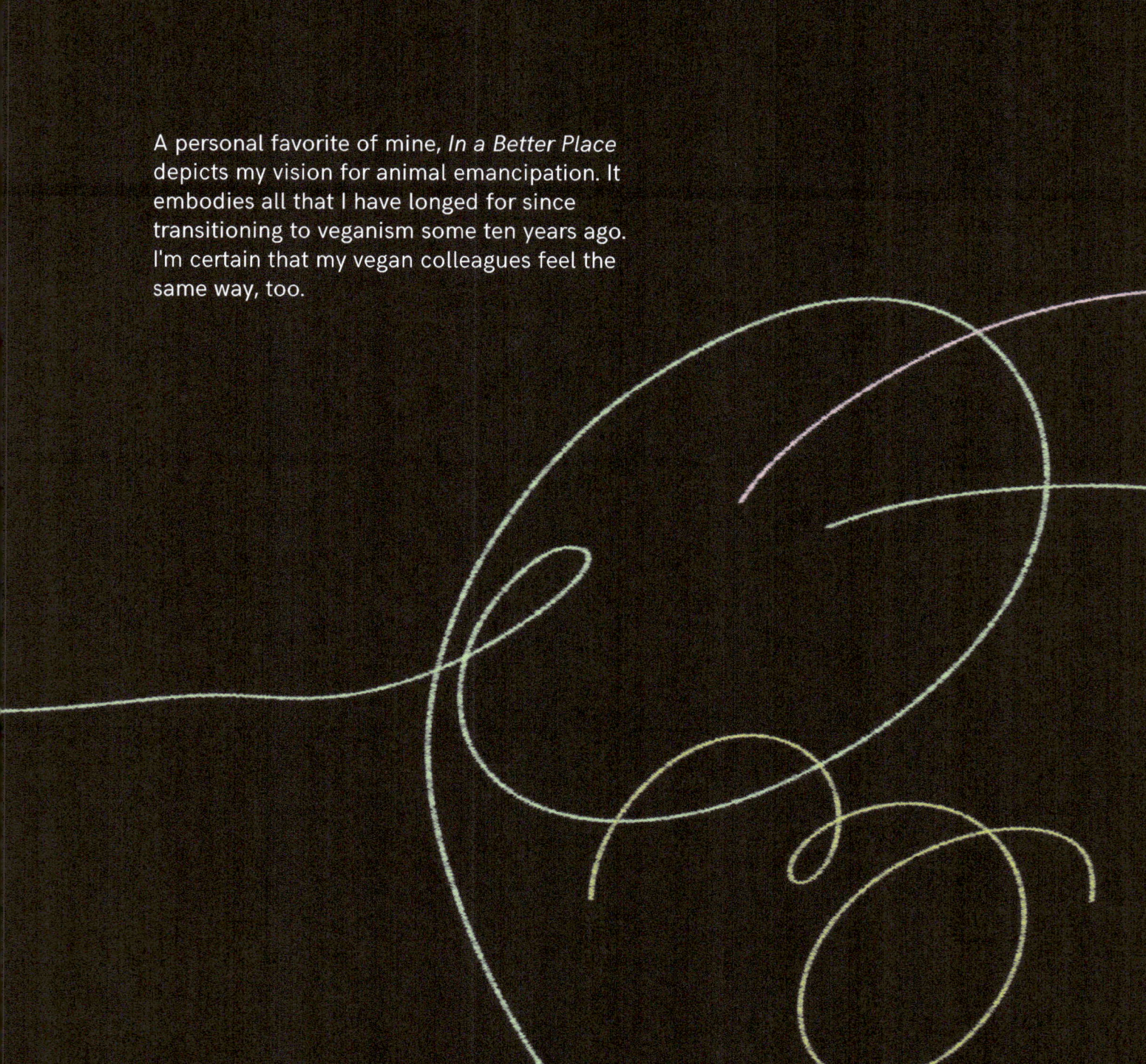

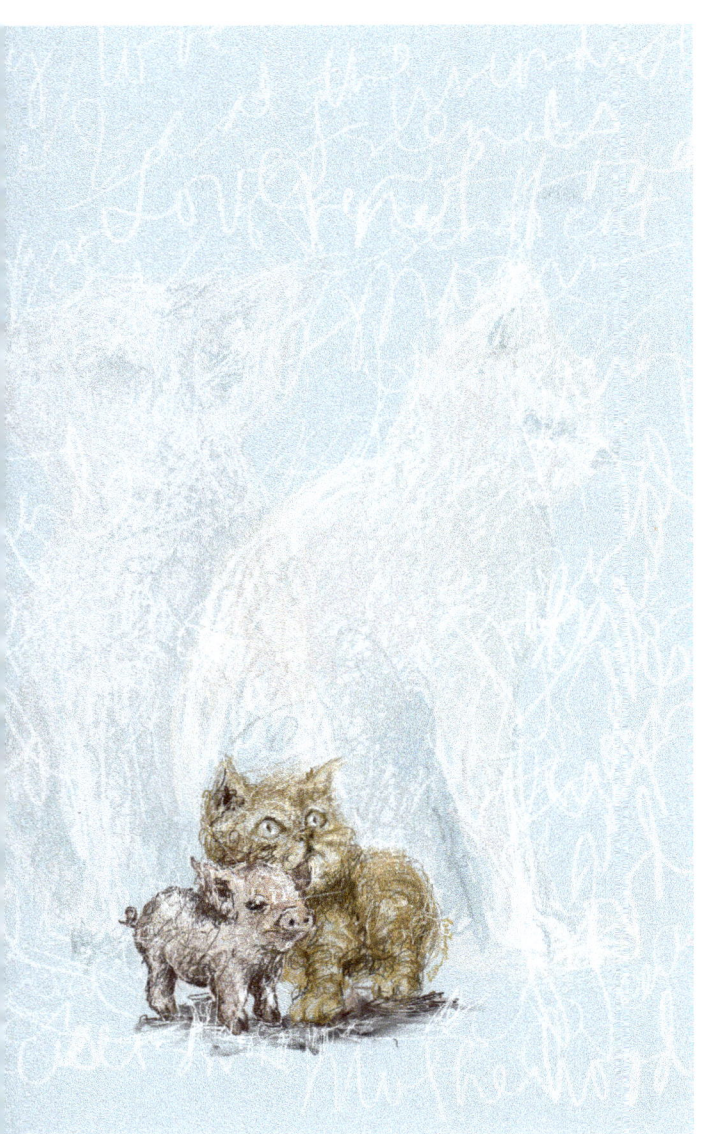

**GENTLE LULLABIES**
11.69 x 16.53 in

**WAITING FOR A BETTER HOME**
8.26 x 11.69 in

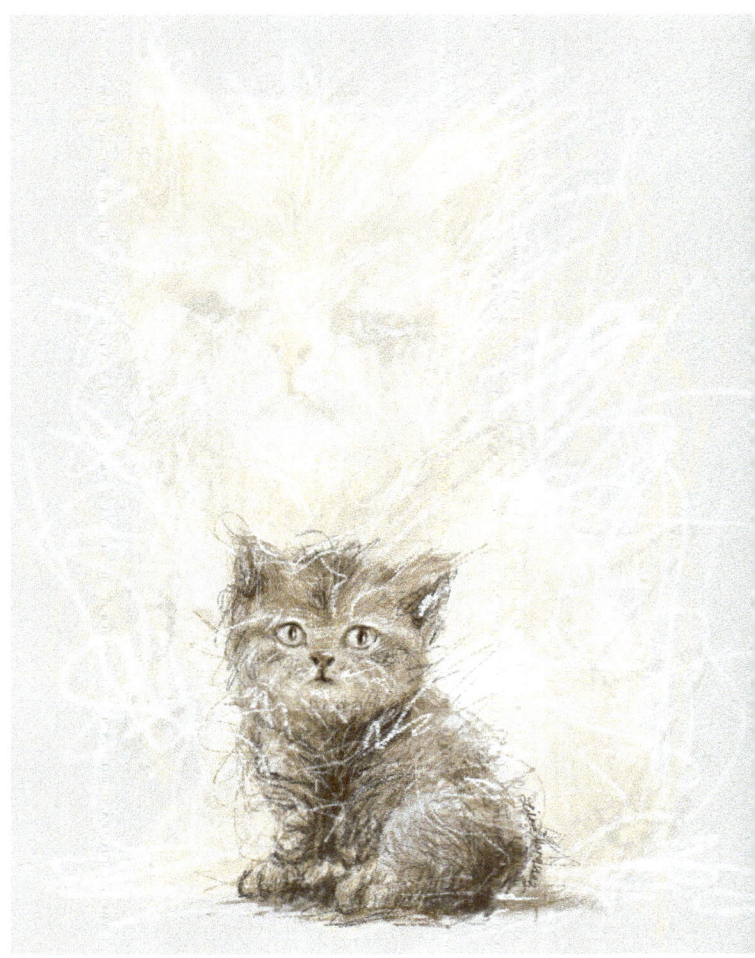

*Gentle Lullabies* is an attempt at addressing the issues of speciesism. In general, it is a part of a series of line painting on orphaned animals.

*Waiting for a Better Home* is a digital painting with a multilayered theme. It is particularly my way of paying homage to my first ever adopted cat, Choco.

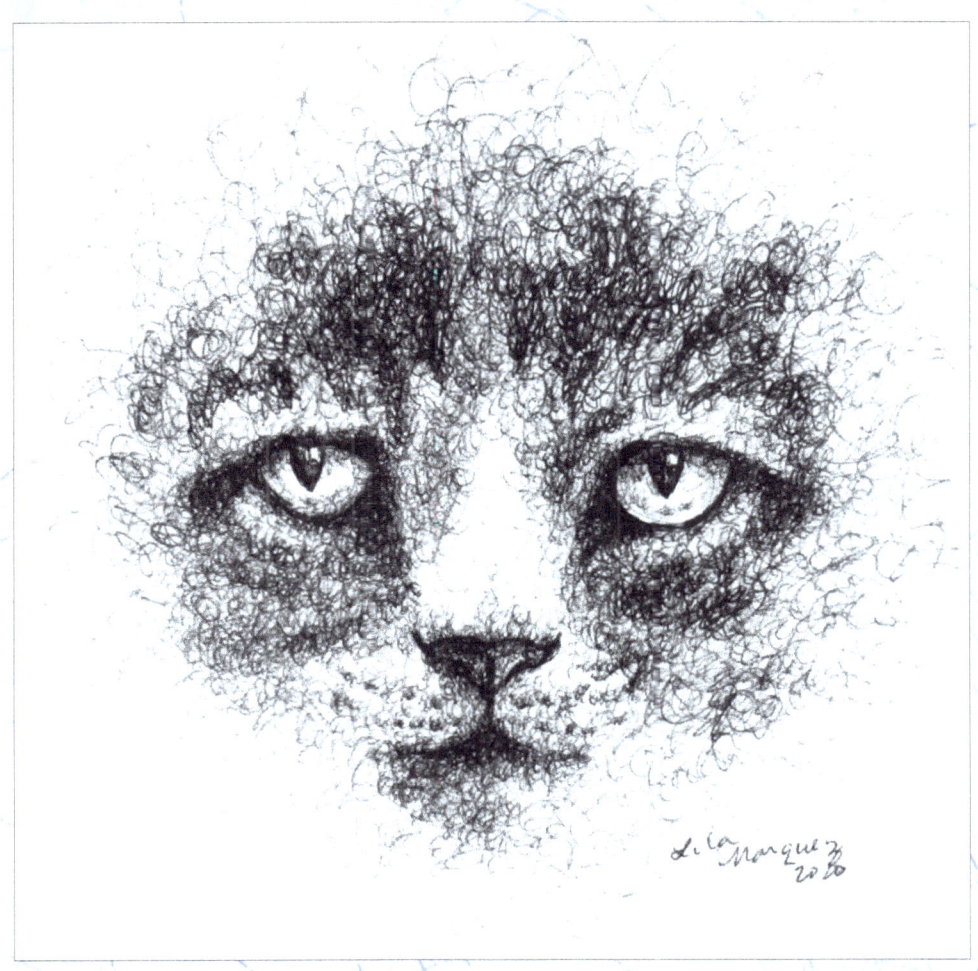

REMEMBERING ALF
5.8 × 8.3 in

*Remembering Alf* is a scribble art inspired by Alf, my cat who passed away years ago. Alf's from-feral-to-family adventure was in 2012 when I rescued him from the street as a kitten and named him Bayn Alfardo "Alf" P. Therpell. We lived in a hostile neighborhood, endured personal predicaments and put up against animal abusers despite his many health complications.

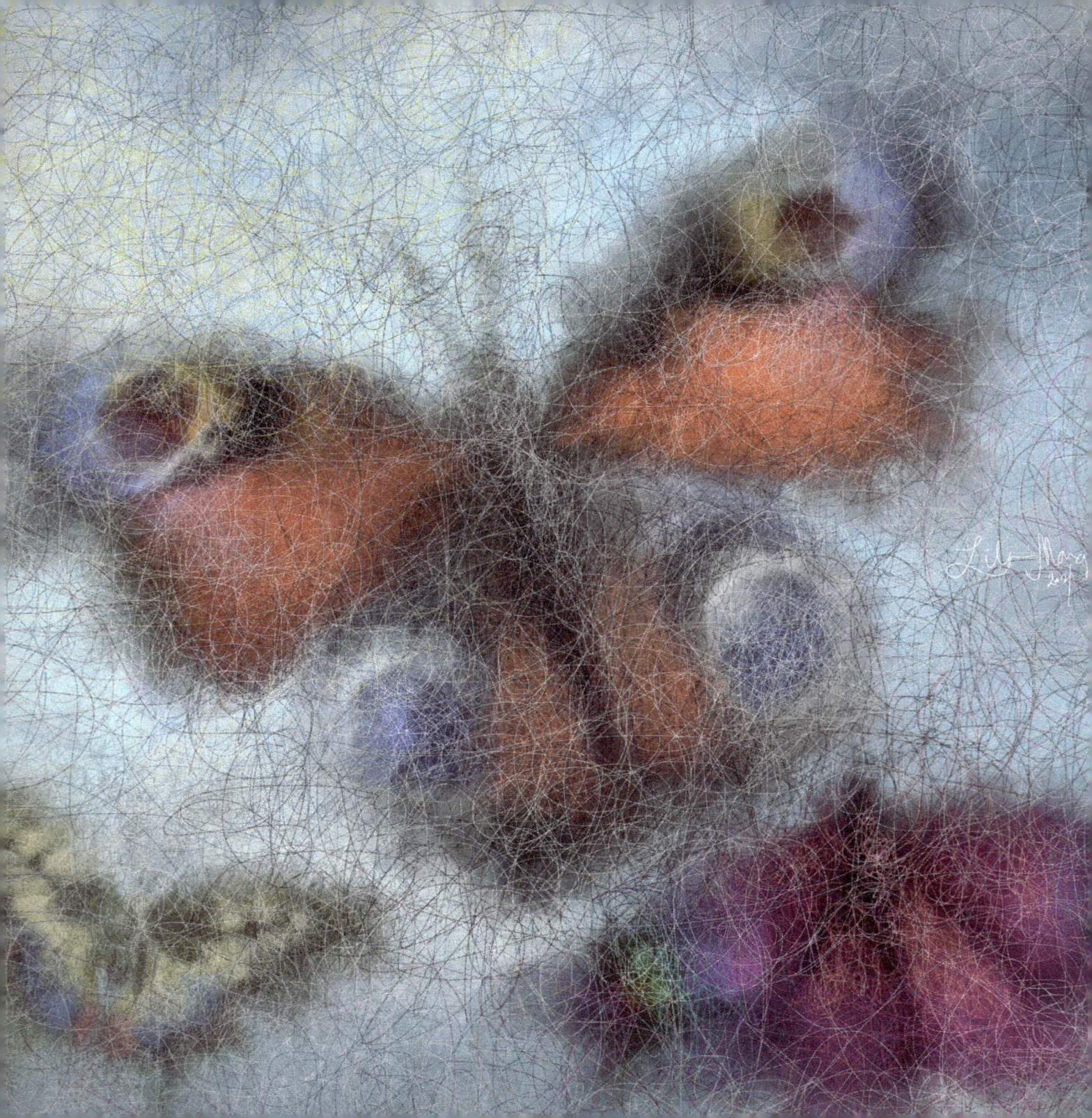

HOPE FOR THE ANIMALS
30 x 20 in

Advocating for animal rights for over a decade has enabled me to adopt various strategies in ensuring animals' voices are heard. I went about establishing online platforms for vegans in Kuwait, writing about the campaign on magazines and newspapers, as well as, leafleting anywhere I went. Despite the fact that veganism was only taking baby steps in Kuwait a decade ago, making a statement on nonhuman animals' personhood and autonomy was always worth it.

I think it's high time that we face the elephant in the room and be persistent in taking a stance against the commodification of animals.

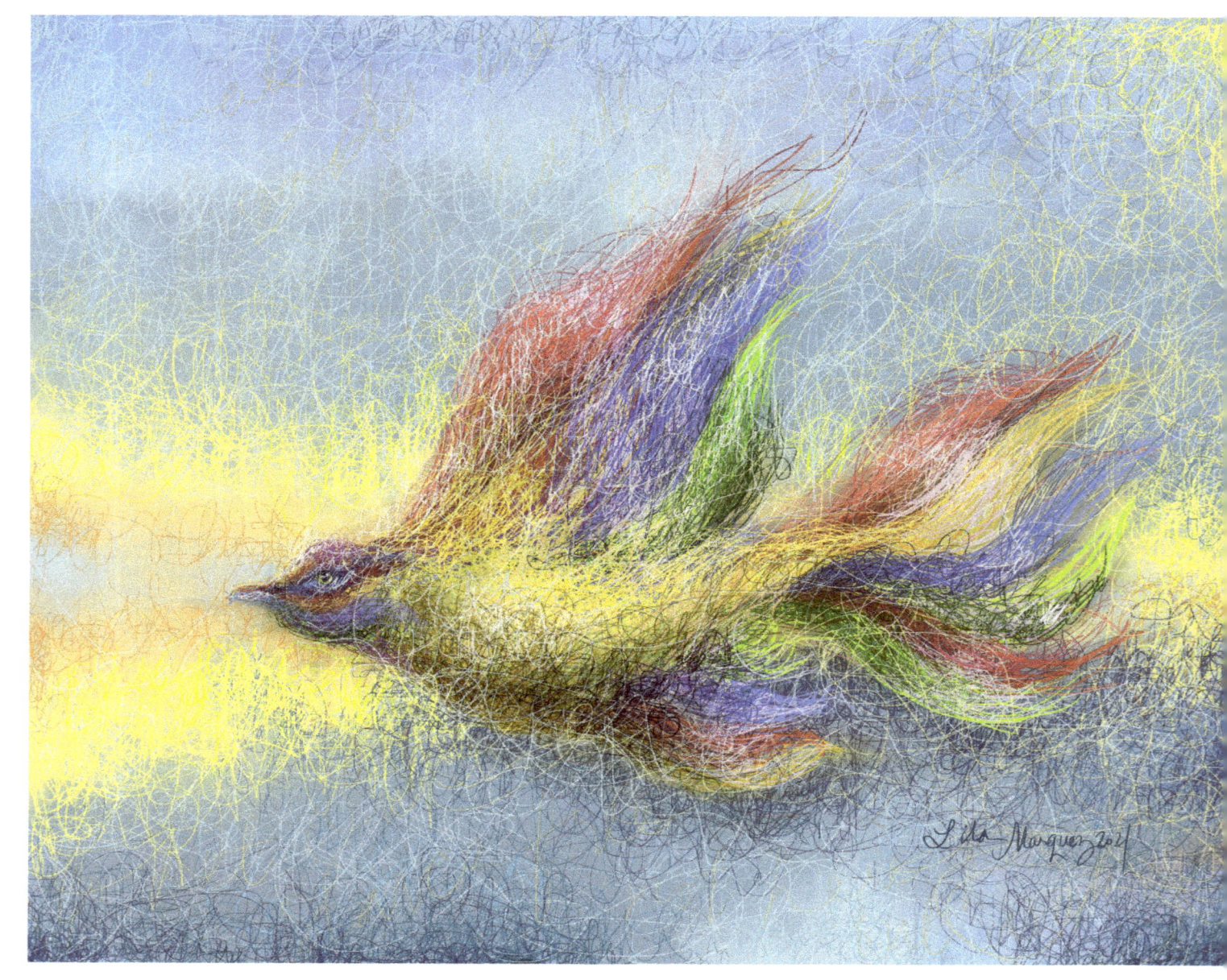

CAGELESS
30 × 20 in

# Sketches

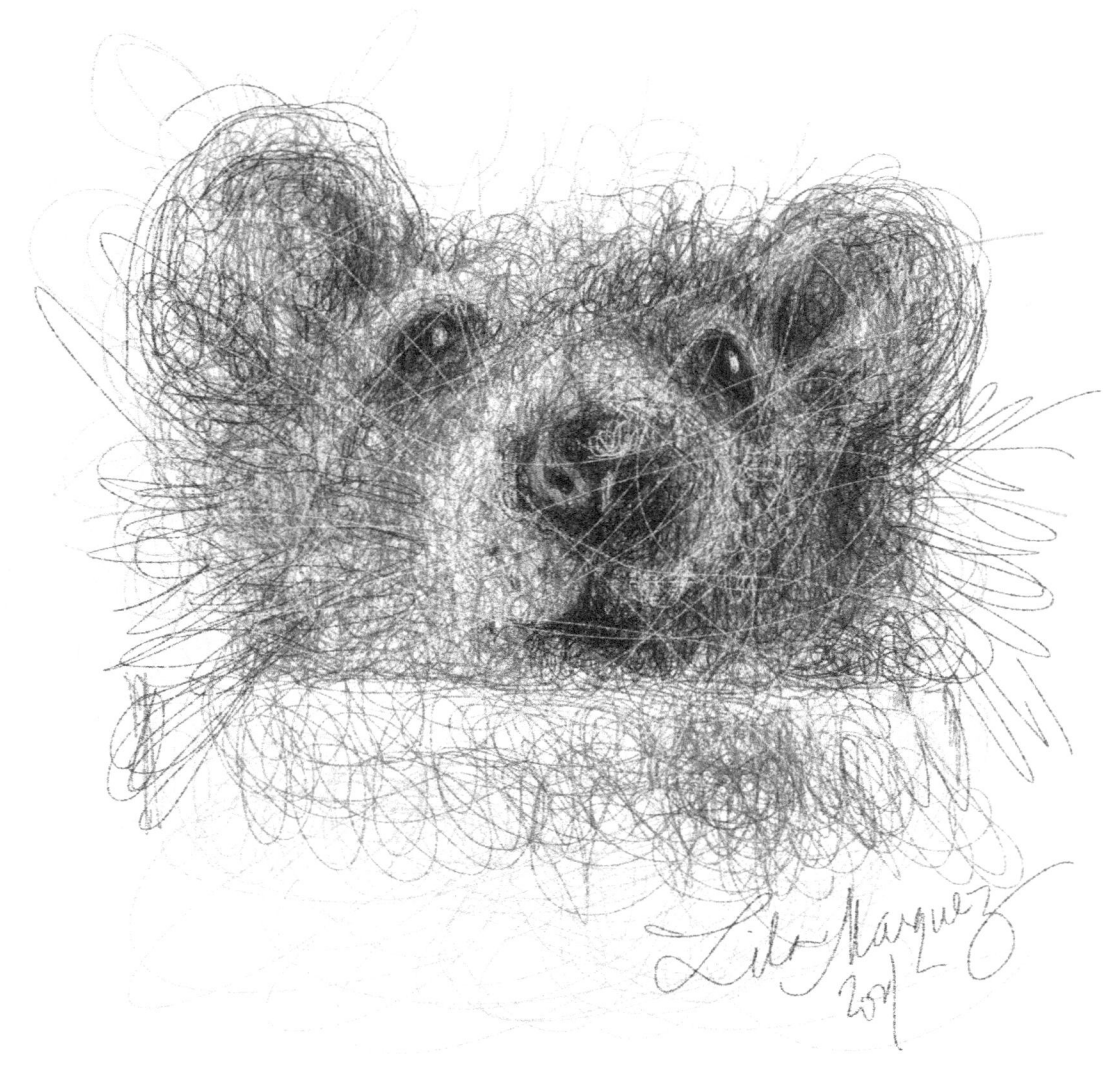

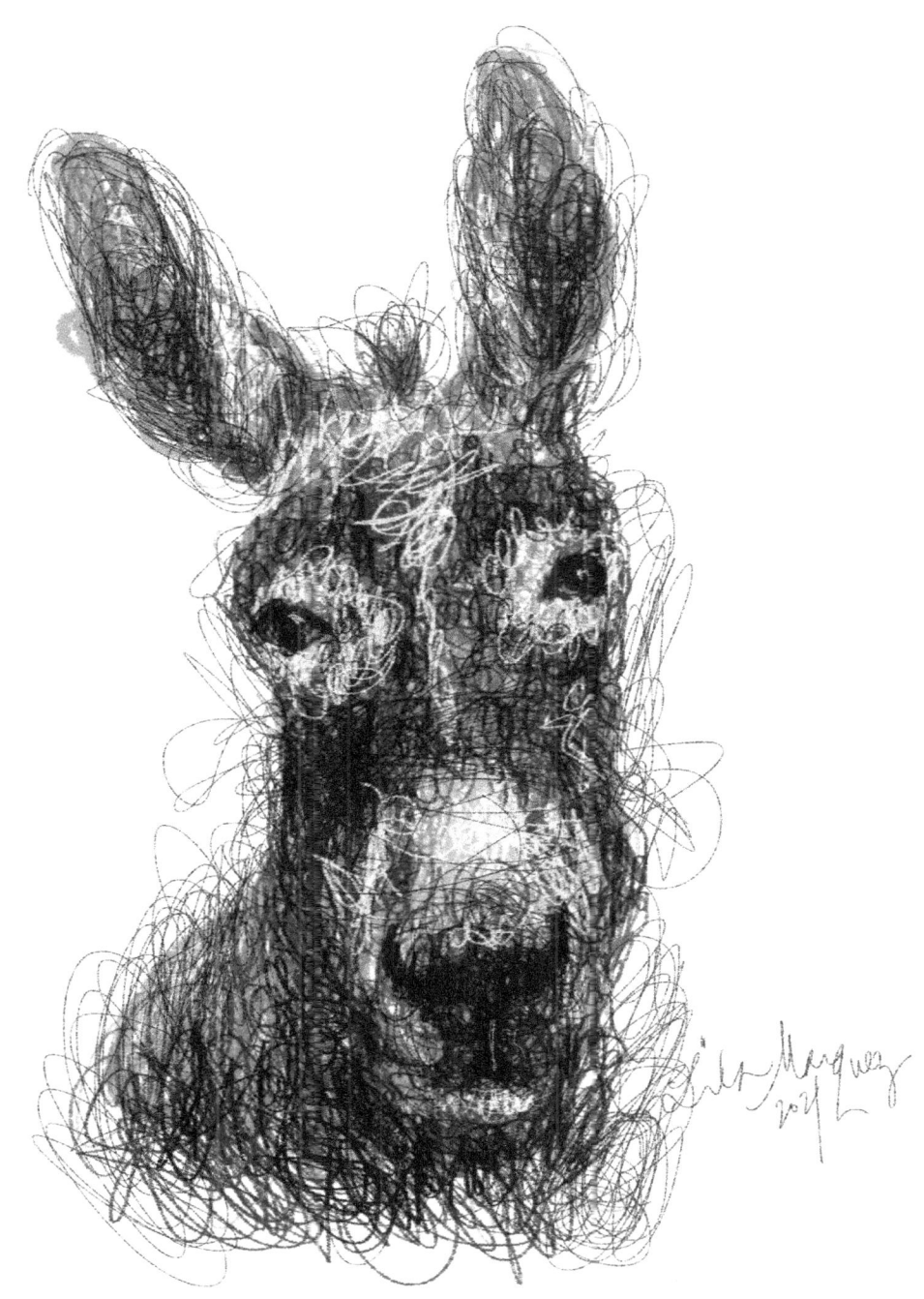

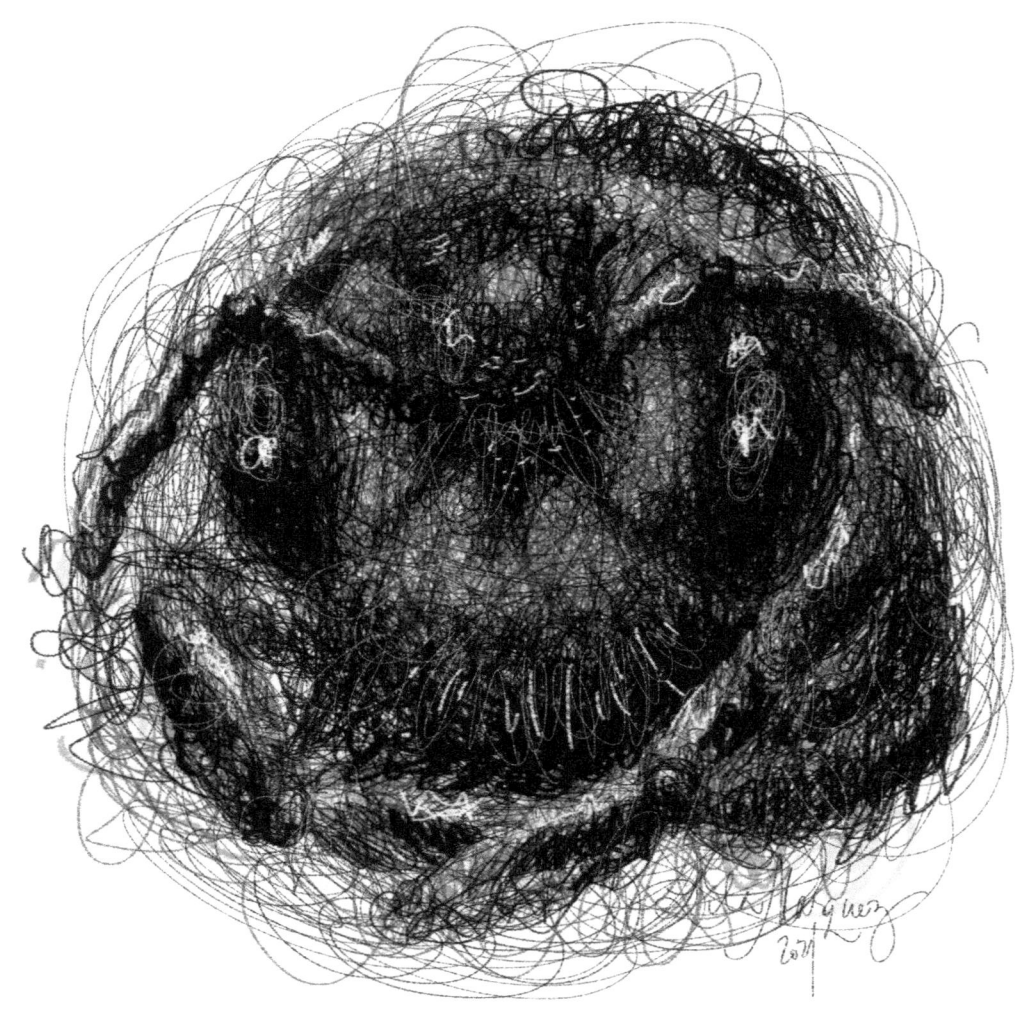

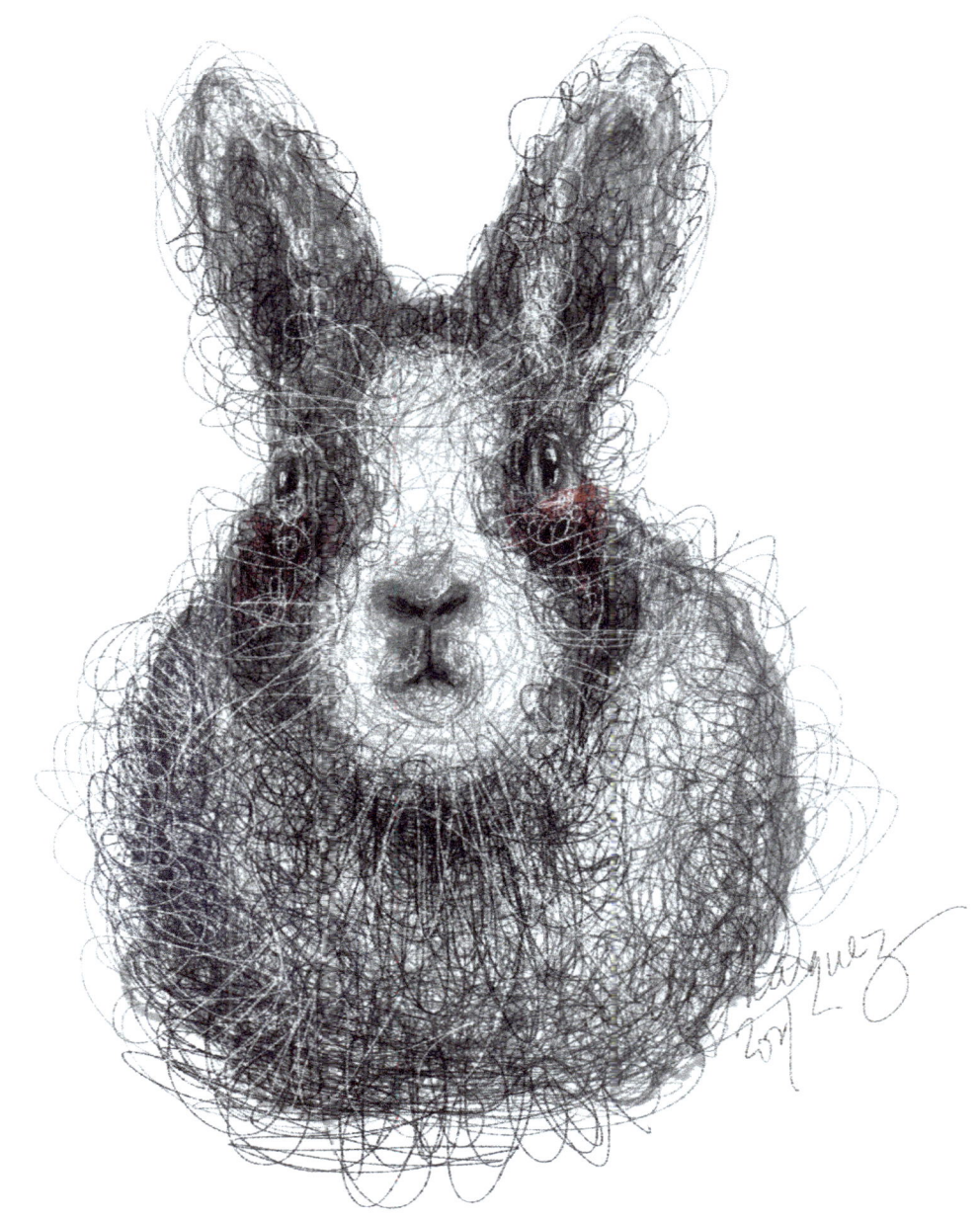

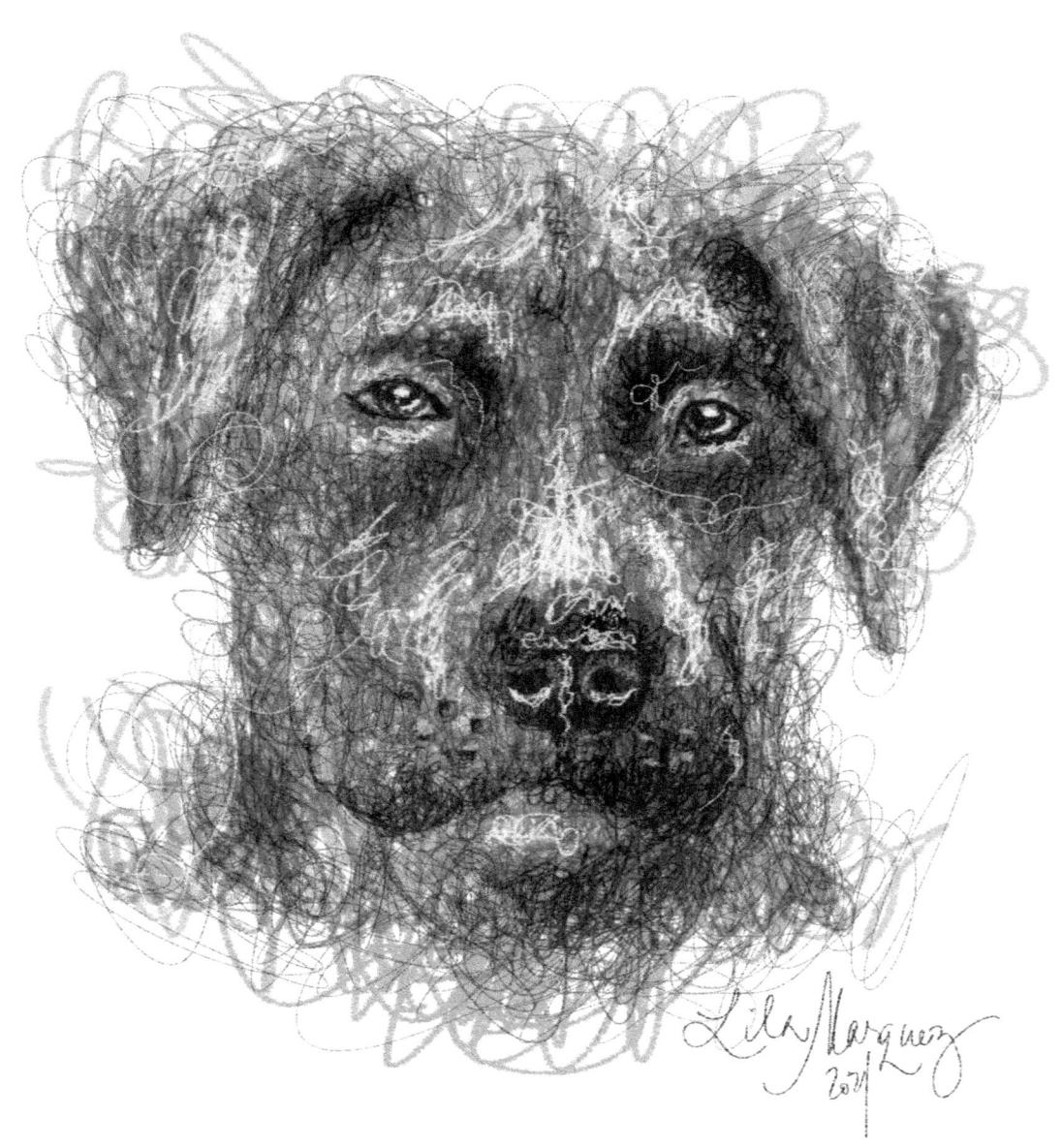

# Break Away

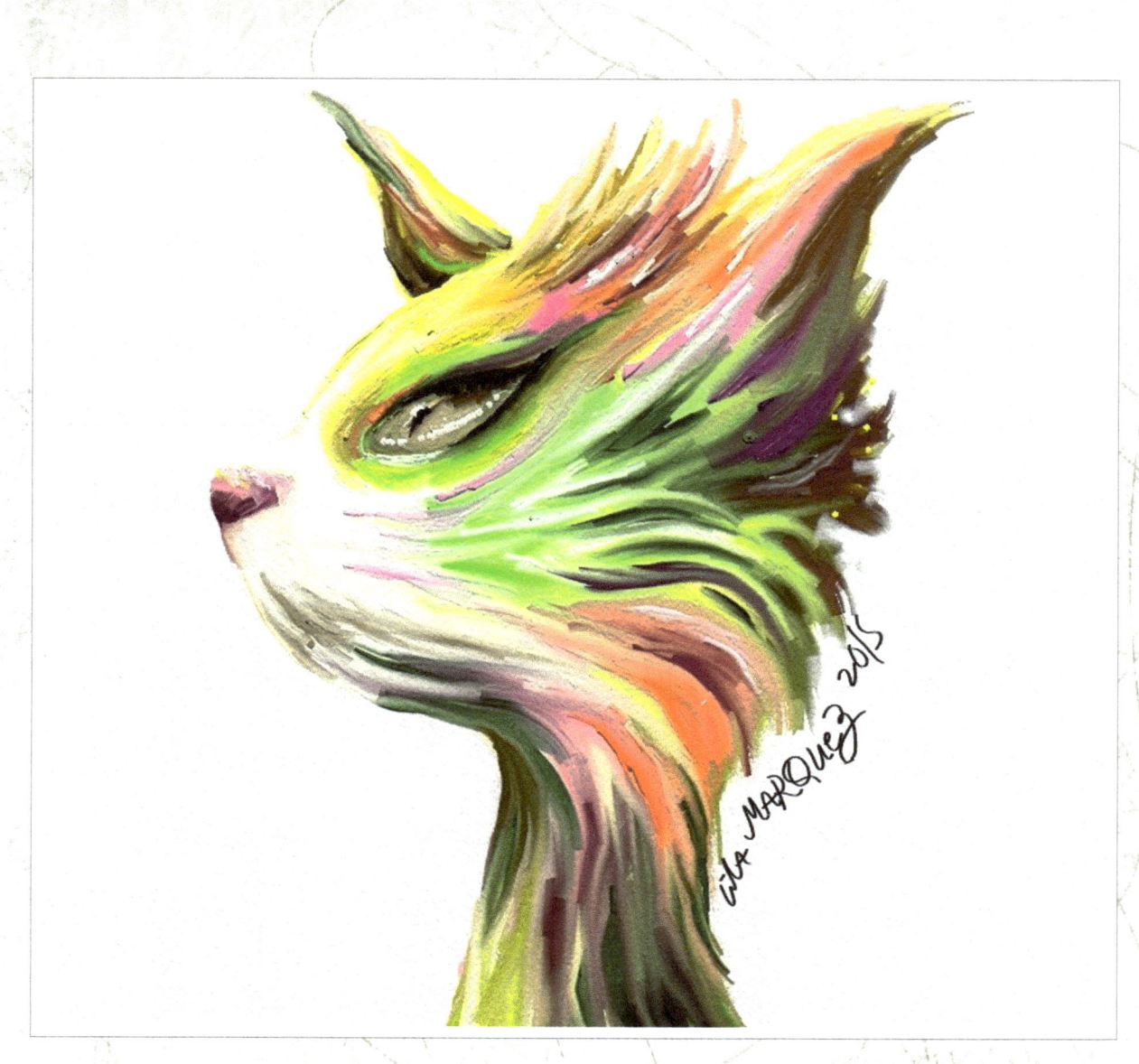

YULI THE CAT
8.19 x 7.35 in

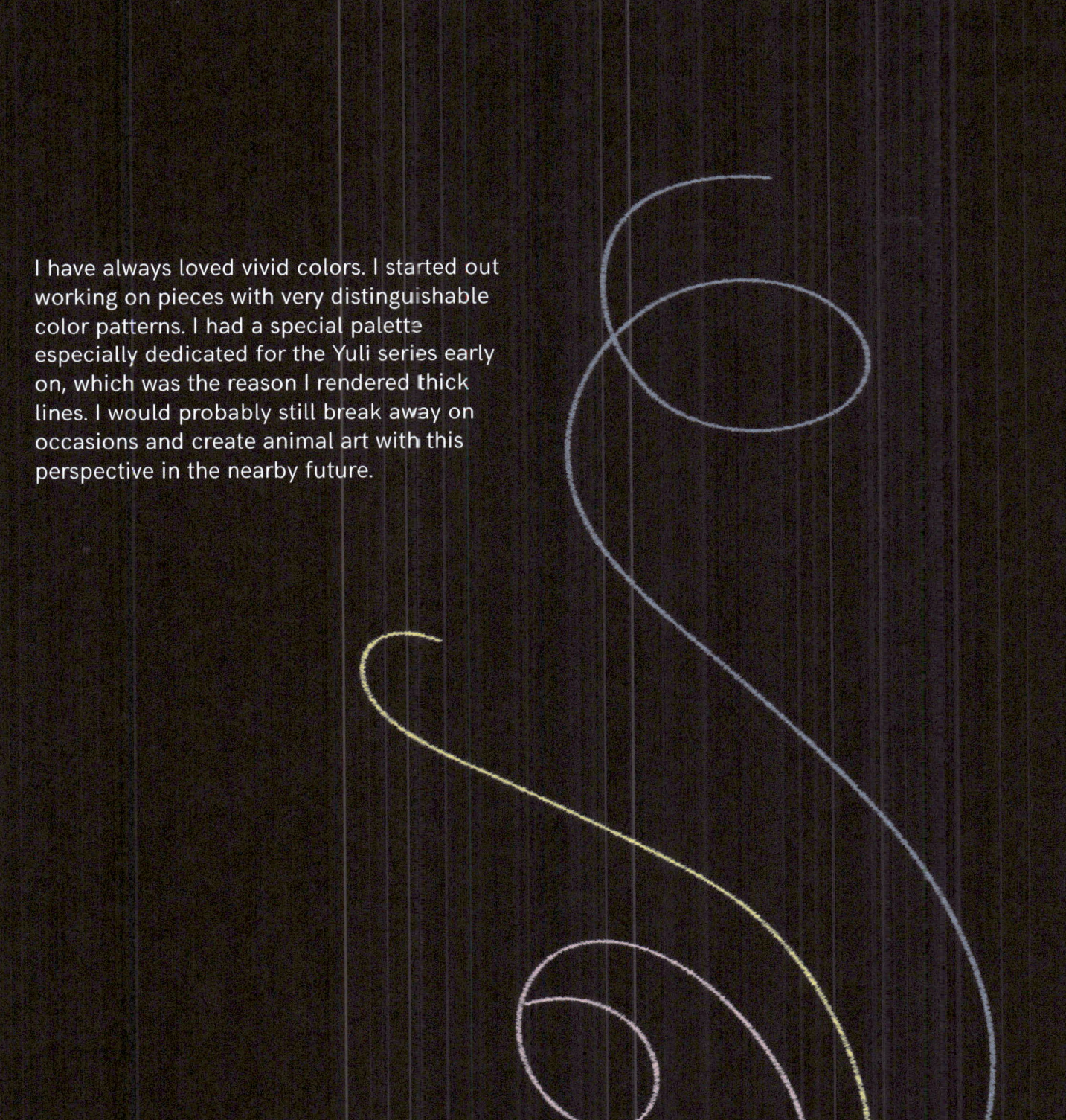

I have always loved vivid colors. I started out working on pieces with very distinguishable color patterns. I had a special palette especially dedicated for the Yuli series early on, which was the reason I rendered thick lines. I would probably still break away on occasions and create animal art with this perspective in the nearby future.

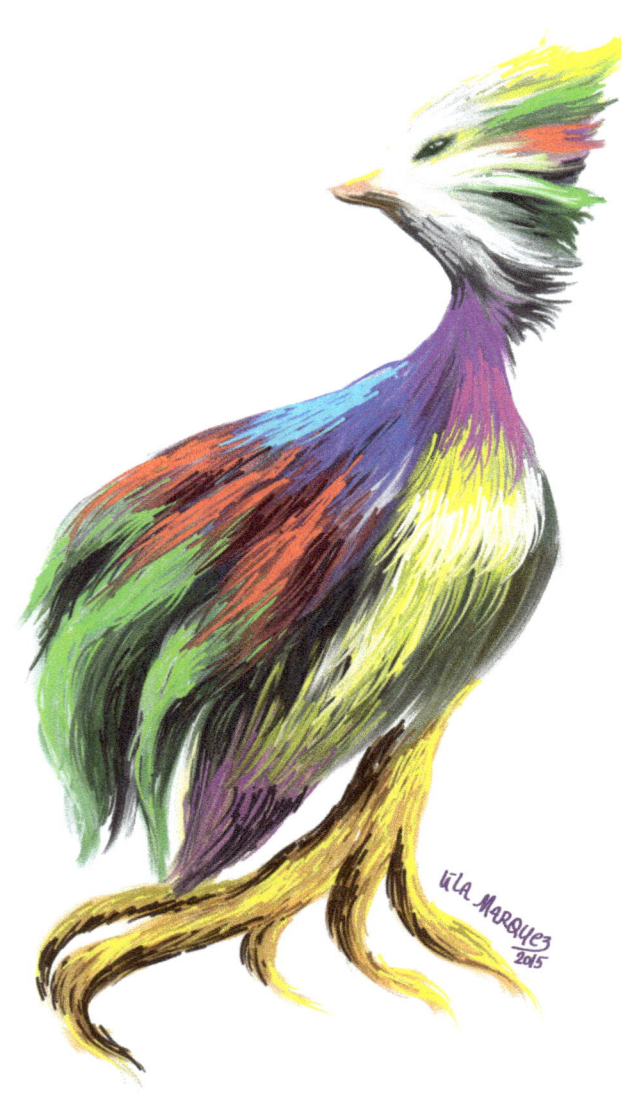

YULI THE ROOSTER
24 x 30 in

YULI THE BIRD
21 x 16 in

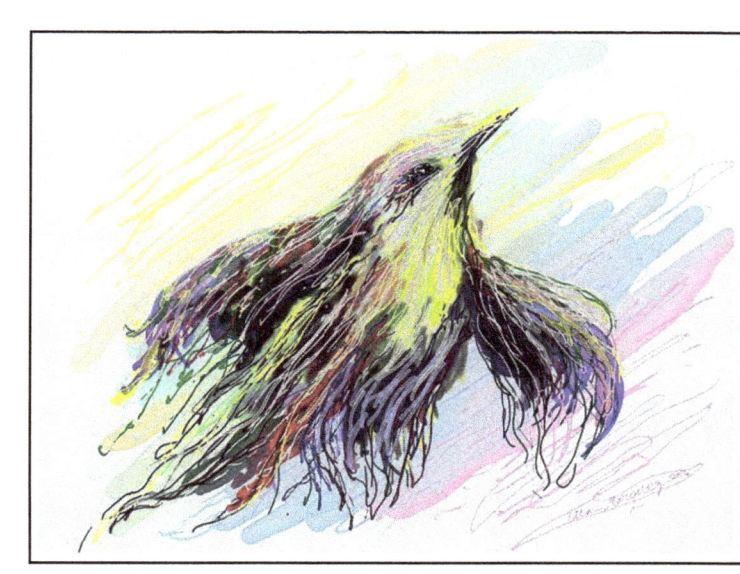

# Exhibitions

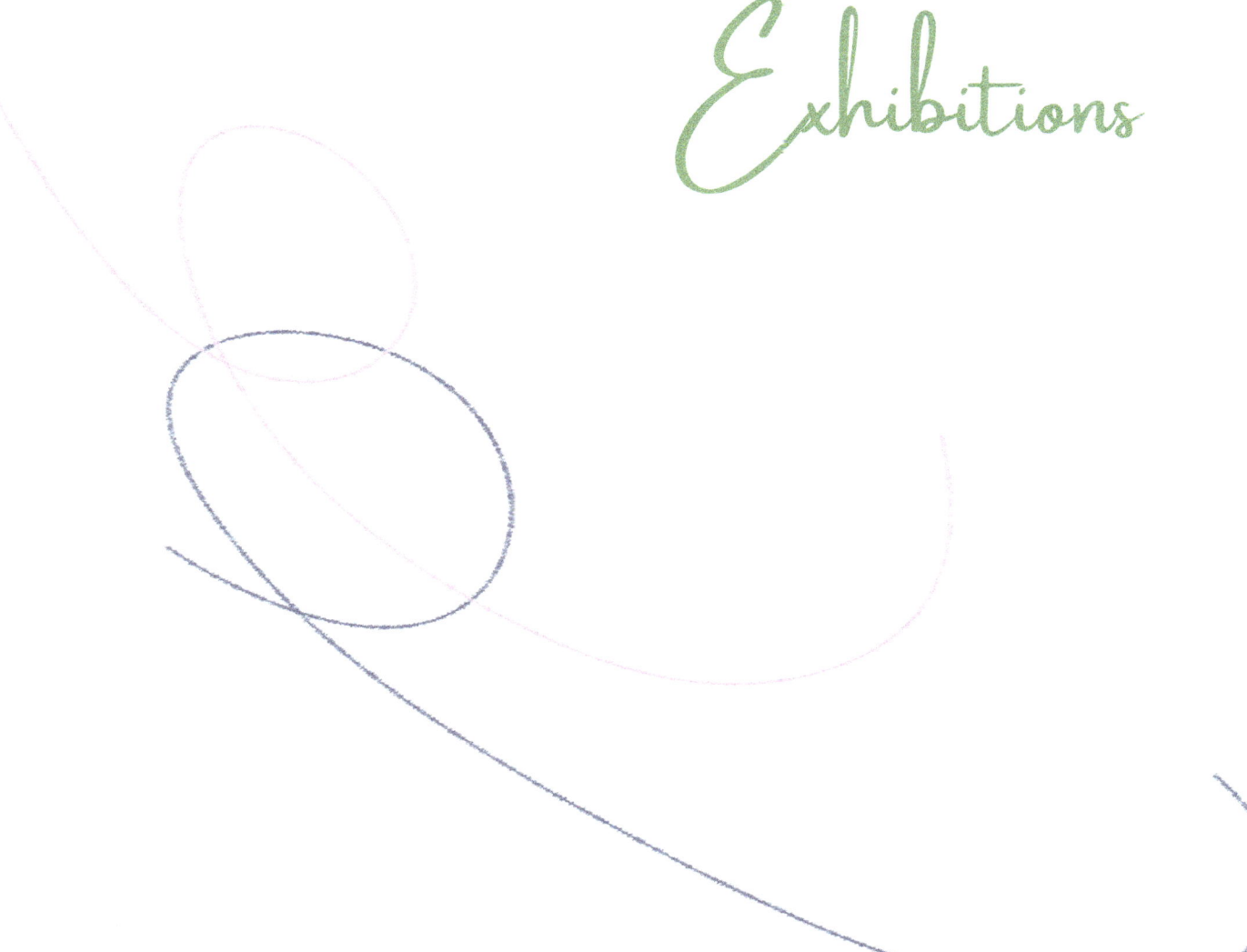

I'm proud to have donated my Animal Art Series to the following exhibitions through the great initiative of The Art of Compassion Project, an international art collective involving vegan artists and raising funds for animal rights causes.

THE TIAJIN CATS PROJECT
Towards a Compassionate Nature (TACN)
1-5 May 2019
Beijing, China

VEGFEST LANCASTER EXHIBITION
Lancaster Farm Sanctuary
1 June 2019
Lancaster, USA

VEGFEST ASHEVILLE EXHIBITION
Brother Wolf Animal Rescue (BWAR)
9 June 2019
Asheville, North Carolina

VEGAN STREET DAY
Vervet Monkey Foundation
8-9 June 2019
Stuttgart, Germany

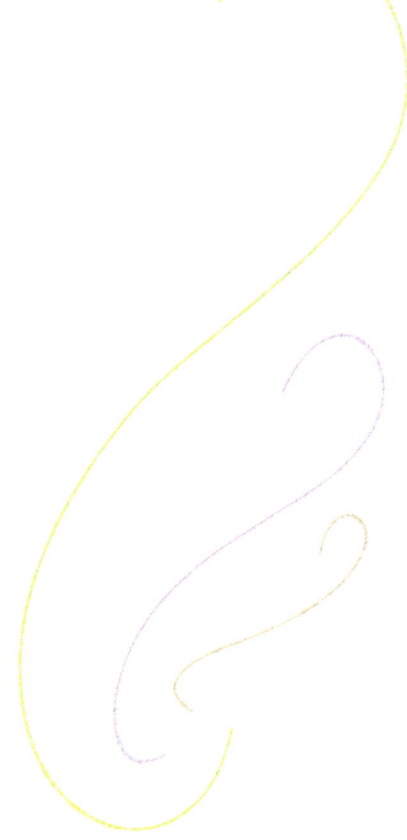

*Exhibitions*...continued

SILENT AUCTION, UK
Animal Equality (UK)
9 July 2019
London, UK

GICLEE ONLINE ART AUCTION
Fish Feel
15 Aug-15 Sept 2019
International (Online)

IARC POSTER EXHIBITION
International Animal Rights Conference (IARC)
5-8 Sept 2019
Luxembourg

VEGFEST UK SUMMERFEST ONLINE EXHIBITION
VegFestUK Summerfest, Vegans Against World Hunger, NSW Hen Rescue
8-22 Aug 2020
International (Online)

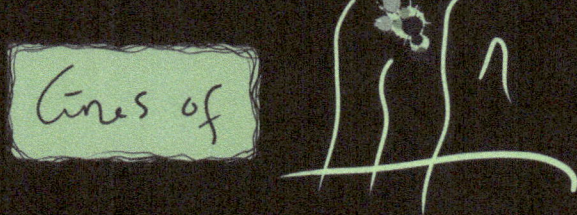

www.linesoflila.com
www.lilamarquez.com

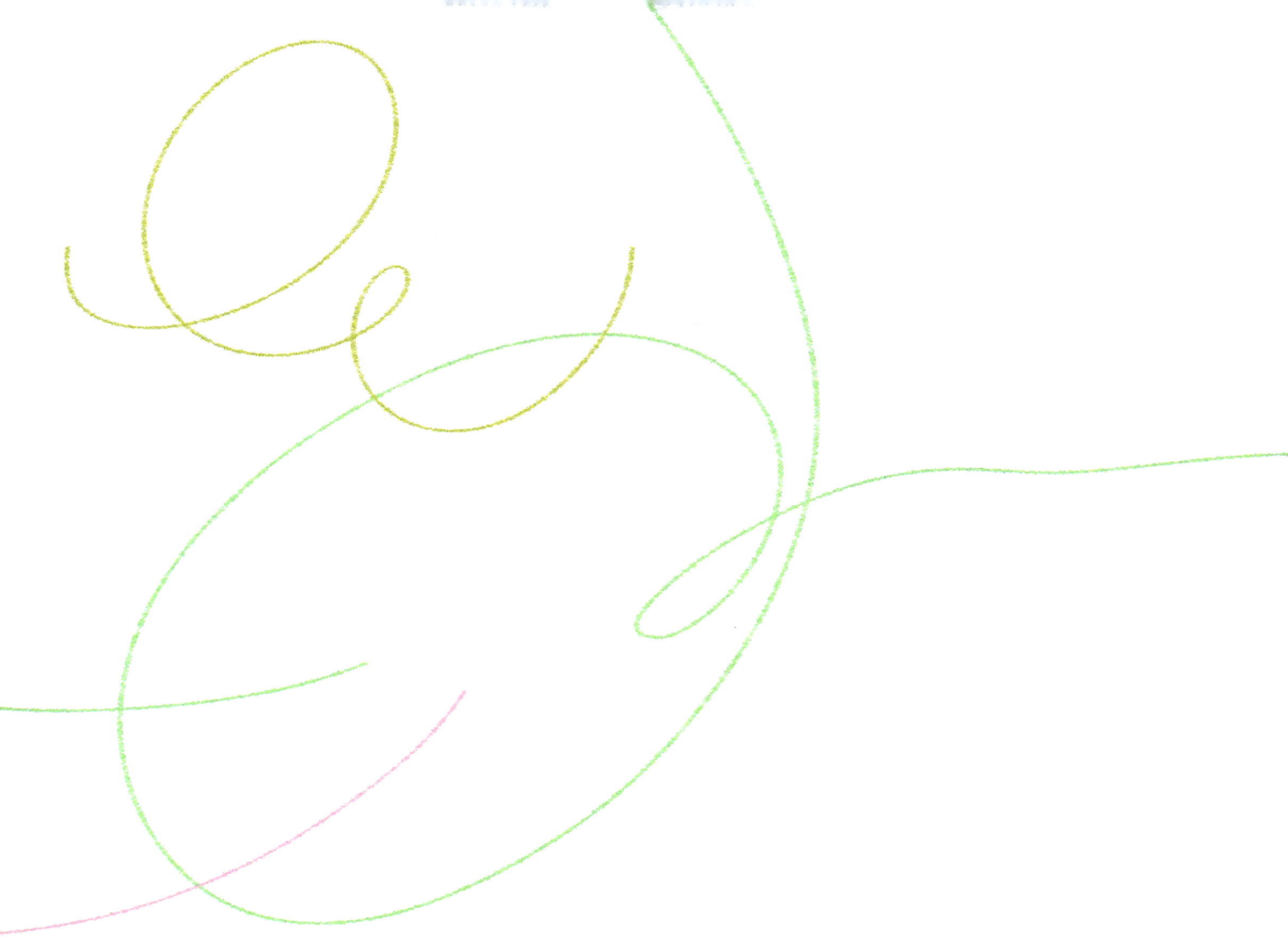

www.ingramcontent.com/pod-product-compliance
Lightning Source LLC
Chambersburg PA
CBHW040547220526
45473CB00017B/3049